MOVIES
A CRASH
COURSE

MOVIES
A CRASH
COURSE

JOHN NAUGHTON
ADAM SMITH

Published in 2003 by Silverdale Books
An imprint of Bookmart Ltd
Registered Number 2372865
Trading as Bookmart Ltd
Desford Road, Enderby
Leicester LE19 4AD

A CIP catalogue record for this book is
available from the British Library

ISBN 1-85605-801-8

This book was conceived, designed and produced by
THE IVY PRESS LIMITED
The Old Candlemakers, West Street
Lewes, East Sussex, BN7 2NZ

Creative Director: PETER BRIDGEWATER
Publisher: SOPHIE COLLINS
Editorial Director: STEVE LUCK
Designer: JANE LANAWAY
Commissioning Editor: VIV CROOT
Edited by: GRAPEVINE PUBLISHING SERVICES
Page Layout: CHRIS LANAWAY, TRUDI VALTER
Picture Research: VANESSA FLETCHER
Illustrations: IVAN HISSEY

Printed and bound in China by

Hong Kong Graphics and Printing Ltd.

The authors are indebted
to David Parkinson for
his valuable advice on
cordwaining.

Contents

Introduction

Mike Myers as *Austin Powers, International Man of Mystery*, set in the swinging 70s.

How this course works

We follow the history of movies more or less chronologically, although each double-page spread is devoted to one genre, or nationality, or director. And on each spread there are regular features. It won't take you long to figure them out.

Everybody goes to the movies. Even if it's only once a decade, some film will come along and drag even the most firmly-rooted couch potato out to the cinema. And more than that, everybody remembers their first movie, and that's something that can't be said of almost any other art form. Try it!

Of course, you don't have to know a great deal about the history of the movies to enjoy a good film. But just knowing a little can enrich your understanding and enjoyment of even the latest blockbuster.

This book provides an introduction to the important people and movements in cinema around the world, like a series of trailers giving you a taste of the delights that

ROLL THE CREDITS

Roll the credits widens the scope, providing name-checks of other movie-makers who worked with those featured, such as screenplay writers, cinematographers or animators; other directors who contributed to or were influenced by the movement being discussed; or actors who helped to realise their directors' visions. And sometimes the relationships between them all – professional and otherwise – are the most interesting part.

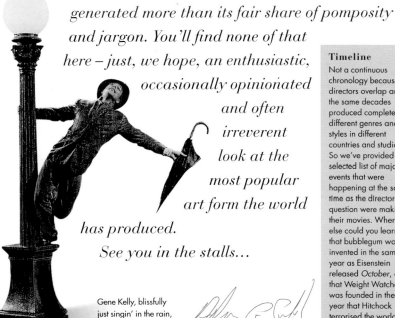

Movie people have dramatic lives on and off screen and tend to trade in their spouses more often than the rest of us trade in our cars. Why was it dangerous to go to parties given by Fatty Arbuckle or Randolph Hearst? What happened to Lana Turner's mobster boyfriend? Who was the love of Clark Gable's life? And which movie actress has had the most husbands? We think you should know.

Lights! Camera! Action!

While you don't want your dinner party conversation to become bogged down in tedious detail, you can seem like a real movie insider if you casually drop references to jump cuts and CGI. We present a few tricks of the trade your friends might not be aware of.

movies can offer: from Eisenstein's Potemkin to Cameron's Titanic or from Frankenstein to Freddy Krueger.

Most importantly we've tried to demystify the whole business of reading about movies. Like any other art form 'cinema' has generated more than its fair share of pomposity and jargon. You'll find none of that here – just, we hope, an enthusiastic, occasionally opinionated and often irreverent look at the most popular art form the world has produced.

See you in the stalls...

Timeline

Not a continuous chronology because directors overlap and the same decades produced completely different genres and styles in different countries and studios. So we've provided a selected list of major events that were happening at the same time as the directors in question were making their movies. Where else could you learn that bubblegum was invented in the same year as Eisenstein released *October*, and that Weight Watchers was founded in the year that Hitchcock terrorised the world with *The Birds*?

Gene Kelly, blissfully just singin' in the rain, from one of moviedom's great moments in film (1952).

ADAM SMITH

399 BC Socrates is sentenced to death by drinking hemlock, accused of atheism and 'corrupting the youth'.

41 BC Cleopatra meets Mark Antony. More than 2,000 years later, the story of their love affair brings Liz Taylor and Richard Burton together.

1499 Amerigo Vespucci discovers America.

*c.*360 BC ~ 1895

Shadows and Illusions
Cinema's Prehistory

Plato, the Barry Norman of his day.

You don't think of Plato as being the first film critic. But his description of the Cave of Shadows in The Republic is the earliest reference to the phenomenon of moving pictures. The ancient Egyptians also took a lively interest. As did the thinkers of medieval China and Arabia, whose studies of light and lenses paved the way for the invention, during the Renaissance, of the camera obscura or pinhole camera.

Science has always played a vital role in cinema. Indeed, it's the only one of the seven arts totally dependent on technology. Even the shadow puppeteers of 8th-century Java needed a light source to tell epic stories of monarchs, magicians and monsters, using elaborately decorated leather puppets. Shadow shows finally reached Europe during the Enlightenment and were still pulling in the punters at Henri Rivière's Chat Noir theatre in Paris in the 1890s.

Similarly, it was a scientist, a Jesuit priest named Athanathius Kircher, who, in the mid-17th century, came up with the idea of projecting hand-drawn images using a magic lantern. Lanternists travelled throughout Europe for the next two hundred years, giving simple shows to princes and peasants alike. The more skilled showmen were soon presenting 'moving' images, by means of mechanical slides and overlapping images, produced

No eighteenth-century dinner party was complete without the hostess putting on a magic lantern show.

by multiple lanterns. The most ingenious show was Robertson's Phantasmagoria, a spooky spectacle staged in a disused churchyard in revolutionary France.

Also popular at this time were novelties like Robert Barker's Panorama and Louis Daguerre's Diorama, in which vast paintings were brought to life by dramatic lighting changes.

All the fun of the movies at the fair, c.1900.

By the 1830s, even kids (or at least the spoilt ones) were familiar with moving pictures, thanks to such optical toys as the thaumatrope, phenakistoscope and zoetrope. They knew nothing about persistence of vision, but then who does? Even modern scientists can't agree on why the brain interprets a series of rapidly moving stills as a single continuous image.

Proving that you don't have to understand science to exploit it, an Austrian baron, Franz von Uchatius, projected the earliest moving pictures in 1853. But it was Émile Reynaud who transformed a novelty entertainment into an art form. In 1892, using the

The first screen joke: an enthralled audience laps up the Lumières' classic, *The Sprinkler Sprinkled*.

Praxinoscope, a contraption comprising a revolving drum lined with mirrors, he presented the first animated films. Each 15-minute 'Illuminated Pantomime' required hundreds of hand-drawn, full-colour images. But, thanks to the experiments of Eadweard Muybridge and Étienne-Jules Marey, his endeavours were about to be eclipsed.

Galloping horses

Eadweard Muybridge (1830–1904), a British eccentric exiled in California, figured out how to photograph movement. His experiments with a galloping horse and a battery of 12 cameras were disrupted when he was charged with the murder of his wife's lover. He finally mastered the technique in 1877, inspiring such imitators as Étienne-Jules Marey (1830–1904), an ornithologist who took remarkable pictures using a 'photographic rifle'.

Muybridge's horse pictures heralded the arrival of the 'movies'.

1895 Oscar Wilde is tried for homosexuality and sentenced to two years hard labour.

1903 Orville Wright makes the first successful flight in his plane, The Flyer.

1905 Intelligence tests are invented by French scientist Alfred Binet.

1895~1914

Roll 'em: Beginnings

The Early Days of Cinema

28 December 1895. Most people are skint after Christmas, but 35 Parisians have forked out a franc to witness the mechanical miracle its inventors, les frères Lumière, are calling the 'Cinématographe'. Once

Louis and Auguste Lumière, brothers in light.

everyone is seated inside the Salon Indien in the swanky Grand Café, a jerky image flickers into life on a screen and some workers can be seen bustling through the gates of the Lumières' photographic factory. At one point, the audience apparently ducks for cover as a train arrives at La Ciotat station – a curious reaction considering moving images had been around in various guises for centuries. It's hardly art. Indeed, it's barely entertainment. But cinema has been born.

Although many tried, no one can take sole credit for the invention of the camera-projector. Some, including *Augustin LE PRINCE* (1842–*c.*1890) and *William FRIESE-GREENE* (1855–1921), made lofty claims but no movies. Others, such as the Lathams of New York and the Berlin-based Skladanowsky brothers, had successfully demonstrated their projectors before December 1895. But it was the Cinématographe that caught on and made *Auguste* and *Louis LUMIÈRE* (1862–1954, 1864–1948) overnight celebrities.

However, the paying public soon tired of endless street scenes, hosepipe jokes and music-hall acts. It wanted novelty and its provider was a magician who'd attended the Lumière premiere. Between 1896 and

1908 10 million Americans go to see films in nickleodeons, so-called because the entrance fee was a nickel.

1912 The infamous Piltdown Man is 'discovered' by an English paleantologist, supposedly providing the missing link between apes and men. It is not exposed as a hoax until 1953.

1914 British, French and German troops build trenches stretching from the North Sea to Switzerland.

1914, *Georges* MÉLIÈS (1861–1938) created hundreds of dazzling fantasies, in which individual tableaux were shaped into simple narratives. The pioneer of trick photography, horror films and costume drama, he achieved international fame with his sci-fi classic *A Trip to the Moon* (1902).

But Méliès merely recorded scenes with a distant, stationary camera. By 1900, more sophisticated methods of screen storytelling were beginning to evolve. At the cutting edge were the Brighton School

The Great Train Robbery (1903) (the first of many burglarized locomotives) was the most sophisticated piece of screen storytelling yet seen.

A Trip to the Moon combined fantastical backdrops with some early special effects.

Captured on Celluloid

The Cinématographe was condemned as arrogant and dangerous after a fire at a charity bazaar in Paris in 1897 killed 121 people, many of them aristocrats. The projectionist was using a mixture of oxygen and ether to heat a small piece of lime until it glowed. The lamp, ironically known as a Securitas, ran out of fuel half way through the show, so they paused to add more ether, then some bright spark lit a match. Early proof that celluloid burns well, and some religious groups claimed it as evidence that God did not approve of this new-fangled invention.

ROLL THE CREDITS

Edison gets the glory but in fact it was his humble assistant **William Dickson** *who invented the Kinetograph camera and the Kinetoscope viewer. Dickson was also responsible for the first film to be censored –* The Serpentine Dancer, *featuring the scantily clad Annabelle Moore.*

film-makers, *G.A.* SMITH (1864–1959) and *James* WILLIAMSON (1855–1933), who pioneered the use of close-ups, moving cameras and cross-cutting between parallel events. These new techniques found their most eloquent expression in *The Great Train Robbery* (1903), the prototype western directed by *Edwin S.* PORTER (1869–1941). Porter was to make an even more significant contribution to film four years later, however, when he hired a ham actor named D.W. Griffith.

1907 Georges Braque and Fernand Léger are founders of the Cubist movement in Paris, aiming to reduce nature to geometry.

1909 30 million gallons of ice cream are consumed in the US.

1920 Rudyard Kipling wins £2 million damages from a firm that had used part of his poem "If" in an advertisement.

1907~1948
D.W.Griffith
The Father of Film

Mary Pickford, Hollywood royalty.

A self-confessed loather of films, David Wark GRIFFITH *(1880–1948) only agreed to act in Edwin S. Porter's* Rescued from an Eagle's Nest *(1907) because he was flat broke. Yet within a year he had directed 61 shorts. By the end of the decade he had transformed almost every aspect of film-making and was being touted as the 'Shakespeare of the screen'.*

You name it, Griffith influenced it. Camera angles, travelling shots, artificial lighting, realistic sets, flashbacks, tinted sequences, split screens, soft focus and narrative devices such as dissolves, fades and irises (expanding or contracting circular masks to reveal or conceal a scene). In truth, he was more a refiner of existing techniques than an innovator, and relied heavily on the genius of his cameraman, *Billy* BITZER (1872–1944). Nevertheless, he did wean screen-acting away from the wilder gestures of the stage, making stars of *Mary* PICKFORD (1893–1979) and *Lillian* GISH (1896–1993) in the process.

During his stint at Biograph, Griffith shot 450-odd films (most of them shorts), including comedies, thrillers, melodramas and westerns, many of which climaxed with a trademark last-minute rescue. But his efforts seemed positively folksy compared to the latest offerings coming from Europe.

Griffith's classic movie ran way over budget, at a cost of $100,000.

1922 Howard Carter discovers the tomb of King Tutankhamun in Egypt and a craze begins for all things Egyptian.

1934 The Catholic League of Decency enforces moral standards on movies to curtail explicit violence and sexual innuendo. Sex scenes have to be played fully clothed and with one foot on the floor.

1948 Fred Hoyle coins the term Big Bang to explain how the universe came into being.

Birth of a Nation

The Birth of a Nation was a huge commercial success but caused riots and controversy with its dodgy racial politics. It tells the story of two families during the American Civil War, one from the north and the other from the south, with the Ku Klux Klan as the conquering heroes who save the day. White actors were blacked up to play roles in which coloured people are portrayed as animals capable of unspeakable atrocities.

A milestone in the development of screen storytelling and technical ingenuity, perhaps, but its director was never going to be nominated for a Nobel Peace Prize. But while it cemented Griffith's reputation, the film's biggest beneficiary was its distributor, a newcomer to the movie business – Louis B. Mayer.

The Father of Film himself, in white panama hat, surrounded by his crew.

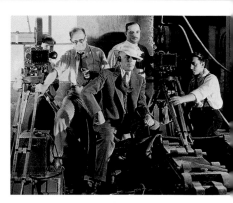

At a time when most movies were aimed at working-class audiences, *films d'art* were a conscious attempt to raise the tone. Adapted from the classics of page and stage, pompous melodramas such as *Queen Elizabeth* (1912) gave cinema social respectability and intellectual credibility. These excursions in turn looked amateurish beside Italian 'superspectacles' like *Quo Vadis?* (1913) and *Cabiria* (1914). Lasting over an hour, these lavish epics turned Griffith green with envy. Following the four-reel *Judith of Bethulia* (1913), he quit Biograph to set about making his masterpiece. Set during the Civil War and running over three hours, *The Birth of a Nation* (1915) was pretty awesome. But it was also unforgivably racist and a storm of protest followed, prompting Griffith to make *Intolerance* (1916) in self-defence.

Cross cutting between four time periods, this complex allegory confused audiences and underwhelmed critics. It was Griffith's first flop and his career never really recovered. Suffocating within the studio system, he increasingly lost touch with popular tastes, and only *Broken Blossoms* (1919) matched his earlier work. He died in 1948, virtually forgotten by the industry he'd helped create. That's showbiz.

ROLL THE CREDITS

Cinematographer **Billy Bitzer** *was Griffith's right-hand man for more than sixteen years, from their first ominously named collaboration,* A Calamitous Elopement *(1908). He was responsible for inventing and developing loads of techniques still used in movies today, including the flashback, softfocus and split-screen shots.*

1896 Georges Méliès' first film, *The Conjuring of a Woman at the House of Robert Houdin*, incorporates magic and film.

1905 Heinz baked beans are test marketed in the north of England and housewives are told they make a nutritious meal for working men.

1914 Archduke Franz Ferdinand is shot in Sarajevo and the First World War begins.

1896~1918

Hooray for Hollywood
The Trust Wars

Thomas Ince set up his own studio and made mostly westerns.

For much of cinema's first decade, everything good was stamped 'Made in France'. The Pathé brothers dominated the business side, while the chase comedies of Ferdinand ZECCA (1864–1947), crime serials of Louis FEUILLADE (1873–1925) and diverse delights of Georges Méliès and the first woman director Alice GUY (1873–1968) rang box-office bells. Producers around the world imitated slavishly. But the Americans were too busy suing and shooting each other to bother much about movie-making.

Miffed at having misjudged the potential of 'flickers', the legendary inventor *Thomas EDISON* (1817–1931) was determined to monopolize the growing American industry. Having beaten Thomas Armat and Francis Jenkins to the patent for their Vitascope projector, he claimed exclusive rights to the Latham Loop, a device that prevented film from snapping inside the camera. In 1897 Armat took him to court, launching the 12-year Patents War, which only ended when Edison called a truce to tackle film piracy.

Distributors appeared around 1905 to act as brokers between the producers and the new nickelodeon bosses. But in the spirit of free enterprise, they also began pirating the latest hits and creaming off the profits. In 1908 Edison and his fellow producers formed the Motion Picture Patents Company and threatened to

1915 In Chicago, 40,000 people protest at a new law closing bars on Sundays.

1916 Home refrigerators go on the market at $900 each, but not many people buy them, since it is possible to buy a car for the same price.

1918 Ripley's cartoon strip *Believe it or Not* is launched, showing men setting unlikely world records.

blacklist anyone dealing in dupes. In response distributors such as *Carl LAEMMLE* (1867–1939), *William Fox* (1879–1952) and *Adolph ZUKOR* (1873–1976) went 'independent' and made their own films.

As the Trust War raged, the MPPC hired armed gangs to disrupt indie production. Movie myth has it that Hollywood was only chosen as a base because it was close enough to Mexico for non-Trust directors to slip across the border before the bully boys could catch them. In fact it offered endless sunshine, varied scenery, cheap land and plentiful labour, but where's the romance in that? Ironically, it was the independents who won the day, their companies forming the basis of the Hollywood studio system. The film factory was the idea of *Thomas INCE* (1882–1924), but it was the group of Jewish entrepreneurs known as the 'movie moguls' who were to cash in on it.

Lasky, Zukor, Goldwyn, DeMille and Kaufman.

TINSEL TALK

Thomas Ince died in mysterious circumstances after a party on the yacht of news tycoon William Randolph Hearst (on whom Orson Welles based Citizen Kane). When Ince collapsed, the official line was that he had indigestion. But rumours spread that he'd been shot in the stomach by Hearst, who mistook him for Charlie Chaplin, whom he suspected of having an affair with his mistress, the actress Marion Davies. Ince's body was cremated without an autopsy.

ROLL THE CREDITS

Many of the best-known producers were already involved in the business by the First World War. **Samuel Goldwyn** *(born Goldfish) produced such key films as DeMille's* The Squaw Man *(1914) before he was bought out by* **Adolph Zukor** *and his partner* **Marcus Loew.** *Zukor next hooked up with* **Jesse Lasky,** *while Loew acquired Metro Pictures from Goldwyn, and teamed with* **Louis B. Mayer.** *In the midst of all this confusion emerged those two Hollywood power players –* Paramount *and* MGM.

1914 The world's first elastic bra is pioneered by Mary Jacob Phelps of New York. She tries it on her maid first before wearing it herself.

1917 Chaplin films are a favourite when shown to soldiers fighting in the front lines of the Great War.

1920 Alcohol is prohibited across the US and sales of coffee and soft drinks soar alongside homemade bathtub gin.

1910s to the 1930s
Slapstick
The Silent Clowns

Chaplin was born in London.

A tramp in a bowler hat and baggy pants hurtles through a revolving door, pausing only to kick his pursuer up the backside. The front of a house collapses, yet the stone-faced man in the doorway remains unharmed. A get-up-and-go daredevil hangs from the hands of a high-rise clock. A pair of natural-born losers try to make some quick cash only to start the mother of all custard pie fights. It's fast, it's funny, it's slapstick.

Ever since a kid soaked a gardener with a hosepipe in a Lumière short, comedy has been a sure-fire audience pleaser. The frantic gag-a-minute style was the brainchild of Mack Sennett, whose Keystone Kops were little more than unbreakable objects, capable of emerging unscathed from any number of pratfalls, chases, assaults or collisions.

Sennett's greatest discovery was Charlie Chaplin, who was plucked from the vaudeville obscurity in 1912 to become the world's first screen superstar. His little tramp films soon began to blend sentiment and social message into features such as *The Gold Rush* (1925) and *Modern Times* (1936).

While Chaplin's style remained rooted in pantomime, Buster Keaton's was totally cinematic. Cutting with unrivalled precision, Keaton constructed gags of gathering momentum that resulted in hilarious pay-offs. Invariably at the mercy of a chasing crowd or such props as a boat, a waterfall or bouncing boulders, Keaton never so much as twitched a facial muscle. He reached his peak in *The General* (1927), released the same year 'talkies' came to Hollywood and put paid to the careers of the baby-faced Harry Langdon and Harold Lloyd, who overcame the loss of part of his right hand to perfect the 'comedy of thrills' in films like *Safety Last* (1923).

Stan and Ollie getting into another fine mess.

1923 Tokyo and Yokohama are destroyed by a massive earthquake and the subsequent fires. 142,807 people are killed or reported missing.

1927 The Cyclone roller coaster opens on Coney Island; it speeds screaming passengers over nine hills for a cost of 25 cents.

1930 *The Shoemaker's Prodigal Wife (La Zapatera Prodigiosa)* by Federico García Lorca opens at Madrid's Teatro Español.

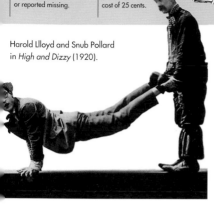

Harold Llloyd and Snub Pollard in *High and Dizzy* (1920).

ROLL THE CREDITS

Who'd be a comic? **Fatty Arbuckle** *lost everything in one night.* **Mabel Normand**, *often teamed with Chaplin, became addicted to drugs and was implicated in the unexplained murder of Paramount director* **William Desmond Taylor**. *The cross-eyed* **Ben Turpin** *and the dapper* **Charlie Chase** *faded out with sound, while* **Buster Keaton** *hit the bottle as he slipped into minor supporting roles. Even* **Chaplin** *himself was subjected to paternity suits, broken marriages and political harassment. A cliché it may be, but there are invariably tears in the eyes of the clown.*

'Fatty' Arbuckle

Roscoe 'Fatty' Arbuckle threw a 48-hour party in September 1921, to celebrate his new contract with Paramount. By the end of it, a young actress Virginia Rappe was dead. Doctors diagnosed acute peritonitis caused by a ruptured bladder. Friends claimed that Fatty had raped her, or at least tried to, and her dying words seemed to implicate him.

Eventually Fatty was exonerated by the jury on all counts but by that time he had lost his house, his car, his contract with Paramount and all his films were withdrawn from circulation. A comeback as William B. Goodrich got him nowhere.

Sound was the missing ingredient as far as Laurel and Hardy were concerned. They were teamed by Hal Roach at the fag end of the silent era. Yet, they retained their flair for physical comedy in the two-reelers of the 1930s, as bulky, bullying Ollie and childlike, spiteful Stan brought chaos wherever they went. Watch *The Music Box* (1932). There's

Buster Keaton and Fatty Arbuckle made a series of shorts together between 1917 and 1919.

verbal wit here. But what matters are the props, which they use to throw, trip over, destroy or simply hit each other with.

Odd comics have since had a bash at slapstick. But no one has come close to matching the genius of the silent clowns.

1915 The long-distance telephone service between New York and San Francisco opens.

1921 The term 'robot' is invented by Czech playwright Karel Capek in his play *R.U.R.*

1923 The Milky Way chocolate bar is launched by Frank C. Mars and named after a distant star galaxy.

1910s to the 1920s
Megalomaniacs with Megaphones
The Directors

Calling the shots.

Striding across the Paramount lot is a man in riding breeches and a shirt unbuttoned to the chest. He's snapping a riding crop into the crisp leather of his knee-length boots. Coarse, flamboyant and extravagant, Cecil B. DeMille is Hollywood's Number One Purveyor of Sin. Across town, an émigré Austrian is boasting about his totally fictitious aristocratic ancestry while polishing a monocle. When he acts, he's billed as 'The Man You Love to Hate', a nickname that whizz-kid studio executive Irving G. Thalberg has recently taken to heart. He's not bad when it comes to Sin, either. But Erich von Stroheim was infinitely more subtle than Cecil B. DeMille.

C.B. was one of the pioneers of the American feature film. Blessed with the gift of knowing what the public wanted before they knew themselves, he flitted from westerns such as *The Squaw Man* (1914) to wartime flagwavers like *The Little American* (1917). Always something of a barnstormer, he came into his own during the jazz age. But although his bath-and-boudoir comedies (*Why Change Your Wife?* 1920) were undeniably slick, DeMille found he could indulge in sex and debauchery to his heart's content in biblical epics such as *The Ten Commandments* (1923), as long as virtue triumphed in the final reel. It was a formula that was to exasperate critics and titillate punters through to his lavish Moses remake in 1956.

Tutored by Griffith, Von Stroheim could never temper his arrogance or curb his instinct for excess. Consequently, he was forever at odds with the studio front office.

Megalomaniac he may have been, but when it came to judging movies, DeMille claimed 'The public is always right'.

KEEP OFF

20

1925 The first part of *Mein Kampf* by Adolf Hitler is published; he dictates it while in prison.

1927 Mickey Mouse is created. He is originally called Mortimer Mouse and his first film is *Steamboat Willie*.

1929 Leon Trotsky is banished to Siberia along with 1,600 followers.

Light! Camera! Action!

Watching Don Ameche in Hollywood Cavalcade or Ryan O'Neal in Nickelodeon, you soon pick up the technique of silent directing. At a time when scripts, let alone storyboards, were almost unheard of, the action often only existed in the director's head before shooting began. As there were no microphones to worry about, directors talked the stars through every move, telling them exactly which gesture or expression to use and when.

Whether booming out instructions to extras in a crowd scene or coaxing a look of love from a temperamental prima donna, the silent director really did call the shots.

Furious at having his savage adultery drama *Foolish Wives* (1922) cut by Universal honcho Thalberg, he swept off to MGM confident of being allowed to indulge his creative urges. But no sooner had he embarked on his masterpiece, *Greed* (1924), than Thalberg was headhunted by Louis B. Mayer and a 42-reel epic was hacked down to ten. Much of what remained was barely comprehensible, but Von Stroheim's genius for mise en scène still shone through.

Tinseltown was a magnet for foreign talent, with the likes of Ernst Lubitsch, Jacques Feyder and Victor Sjöström among the big-name European imports. However, there was no shortage of notable homegrown directors. Admittedly, James Cruze, Rex Ingram, Fred Niblo and Herbert Brenon failed to make the grade in the sound era; but Henry King, King Vidor, John Ford, Alan Dwan and William Wellman were among those silent stalwarts who made a successful transition.

Von Stroheim was often thwarted by the studios butchering his masterpieces.

Mise en scène

How does the director decide what should be seen on screen at any given time during the movie? When should there be a wide shot encompassing the whole of the action and when should he opt for a close-up? Which significant details must be seen? When is it more

Alfred Hitchcock, miseur-en-scène extraordinaire.

important to show a reaction rather than an action? Many of these questions will be answered in the screenplay but some are not finally decided until the editing process. Film students use the term mise en scène (also called mise en shot) in an attempt to impress the uninformed. It actually just means everything that's put in a scene, especially sets, props, costumes, actors and lighting, in order to create the final effect the director wants. The term was also applied to the technique, favoured by the likes of Orson Welles and Jean Renoir, of filming the action in long takes from a moving camera using deep focus.

1916 US President Wilson promises women that they will have the vote 'in a little while'.

1921 English explorers find tracks in the Himalayas like huge human footprints and the legend of the yeti spreads to the West.

1926 Scottish inventor John Logie Baird gives the first successful demonstration of television.

1910s~1920s

They Had Faces Then
The Stars

'All actors are cattle.' The Hollywood moguls of the 1920s might have shared Alfred Hitchcock's opinion, but they knew the value of their stars. The studio heads had recognised the need to pander to the audience tastes by repeating winning formulas. But genres were merely a safety net. What sent a movie into box-office orbit were the names above the title.

The Son of the Sheik (1926), with a swooning Agnes Ayres, was one of Valentino's great popular successes.

In the beginning, screen acting was considered such a last resort that the majority of early performers preferred anonymity. It also meant the producers could pay them less. But Carl Laemmle broke the mould in 1910 when he circulated false rumours of the death of the 'IMP girl' (named after his studio). Florence Lawrence, however, was very much alive and overnight became the cinema's first celebrity.

Hopefuls flocked to Tinseltown, with the lucky few having their carefully tailored

Pickfair

When Mary Pickford married Douglas Fairbanks in March 1920, it caused a sensation for more than one reason. He was the much-loved star with the graceful swagger and easygoing charm; she was America's sweetheart; and together they formed Hollywood royalty, entertaining lavishly at their palatial home, Pickfair. But shortly after their marriage the attorney general announced that she was to be prosecuted for bigamy and perjury after doubts about the legality of her divorce from previous husband, actor Owen Moore. Regally, the Pickfairs left the country for Europe, letting their attorneys sort things out, and for the next decade they attracted huge crowds and stopped the traffic wherever they decided to go. They divorced in 1935 and he later married his English mistress Lady Ashley, but while it lasted the Pickford-Fairbanks marriage seemed to be made in heaven as far as the public were concerned.

1929 Prokofiev's *The Prodigal Son* opens at the Sarah Bernhardt Theatre in Paris, performed by the Ballets Russe.

1931 Academy Awards Director Margaret Herrick coins the name "Oscar" for the statuettes given as prizes because they look like her Uncle Oscar.

1933 Mae West writes and stars in the movie *She Done Him Wrong*, wringing double meanings out of songs such as 'I Like a Guy What Takes His Time' and 'I Wonder Where My Easy Rider's Gone.'.

Genres

Genres were a way of letting the audience know what to expect even before the lights dimmed. Give 'em what they want and then rework the formula before they can tire of it. Most of the main genres were in place by the end of the silent era – comedy, horror, melodrama, the western and action adventures from swashbucklers to war films. The musical came with the Talkies, while sound brought a new edge to the crime picture. Sci-fi was something of a late starter, only capturing the public imagination in the 1950s.

images, whirlwind romances and luxury lifestyles splashed across the pages of the growing number of fanzines.

You paid your money and took your pick. Those not up to being vamped by Theda Bara or Pola Negri could share in the suffering of worldly women like Gloria Swanson. Alternatively, you could sit by the fire with such homely innocents as Lillian Gish or hit the town with flappers like Colleen Moore and '"It" girl', Clara Bow. Hot flushes were provided by Latin lovers like Rudolph Valentino and Roman Novario, while

chaste blushes came courtesy of such boys-next-door as Richard Barthelmess and John Gilbert. Toss in some cowboys, clowns and child stars and that doggy daredevil Rin Tin Tin, and you had yourself a star system.

But the days of glitz, glamour and gossip were numbered. A series of scandals, including the murder of director William Desmond Taylor and the overdose death of actor Wallace Reid, saw Hollywood branded as the new Babylon. Anxious to avoid a government inquiry, the moguls ordered the stars to clean up their acts and imposed a list of 'Don'ts and Be Carefuls' on film-makers. Censorship was skirted by having producers voluntarily submit scripts and finished films to the Hays Office for close scrutiny. But by 1934 a production code was in place that ensured Hollywood remained the right side of wholesome until the 1960s.

Dream Palaces

After fairground tents and amusement arcades, the nickelodeon must have seemed luxurious to moviegoers of the 1900s. Five cents to sit on a hard bench in a room full of chattering people to watch some flickering images was something of a bargain to your average immigrant or worker keen to escape the grim realities of life. But by 1910, longer films had attracted a better class of audience and the great dream palaces were built to give everyone a taste of the exotic. Roxy Rothafel controlled such New York venues as Radio City Music Hall, while in Hollywood Sid Grauman ran the Egyptian, complete with its hieroglyphic décor, and the stillstanding Chinese, outside which is the famous pavement containing the hand and footprints of the stars.

Archetypal Jazz Baby Clara Bow became known as the 'It' girl after starring in a film called *It* (1927).

1917 Russia's Bolshevik Revolution creates a new Council of People's Commissars, with Lenin as the head, Trotsky as commissar for war and Stalin as commissar for national minorities.

1921 Electrolux vacuum cleaners are introduced by a Swedish lamp salesman, Axel Wenner-Gren.

1923 The popsicle is invented by Frank Epperson after he leaves his lemonade on a windowsill overnight.

1917~1930
Montage and Message
Soviet Cinema

What can you do? Lenin has just announced, 'For us, the cinema is the most important of the arts', and yet you don't even have enough film to record him making the speech? For Lev KULESHOV (1899–1970) and his students at the Moscow Film School, the answer was a) to act out the filming process with empty cameras, and b) to re-edit existing pictures – Griffith's Intolerance, *for one. But for directors such as Dziga VERTOV (1896–1954), who were under orders to produce persuasive propaganda, the problem was slightly more pressing.*

October was heavily censored by the Soviet authorities. Trotsky had to be cut from the film after falling from favour.

Ultimately, the shortage proved to be a blessing in disguise. Using every trick in the camera's repertoire, Vertov grabbed snippets wherever he went on his 'agit-prop' train. Cross-cutting the footage with old Tsarist films, he produced over 20 Kino-Pravda ('Film Truth') newsreels, which conveyed exactly the pro-revolutionary energy the Kremlin wanted.

Back in Moscow, Kuleshov was proving the theory of montage – that a film's meaning owed as much to the order of the individual shots as it did to what was in them. Intercut a man's face with pictures of a bowl of soup, a child with its teddy and a corpse and he'll alternately appear hungry, happy and sad. Clever, huh?

Montage was not only a break from bourgeois Hollywood editing, it was also infinitely more subtle. *Vsevolod PUDOVKIN* (1893–1953) showed in *Mother* (1926) how images could be linked to achieve dramatic and symbolic effect, while *Alexander DOVZHENKO* (1894–1956) came close to film poetry with *Earth* (1930), a story about collective farms in the Ukraine.

1924 George Balanchine defects from the Soviet State Dancers while on tour in Paris, and joins Diaghilev's Ballets Russe.

1929 Luis Buñuel and Salvador Dali are welcomed into the Surrealist movement after the premiere of *Un chien andalou*, which opens with a razor slicing into an eye.

1930 Vladmir Mayakovsky commits suicide, disillusioned with the Soviet life he had welcomed thirteen years previously.

But *Sergei Eisenstein* (1898–1948) was having none of that. A devotee of intellectual montage, he believed images should collide into one another to form a 'kino fist' with which to assault the audience. Symbolic imagery flashed across the screen in *Strike* (1924), *The Battleship Potemkin* (1925) and *October* (1927); perhaps the closest anyone got to movie Marxism. However, Eisenstein had changed his tune by the time he made *Alexander Nevsky* (1938) and *Ivan the Terrible* (1942–1944), which laid greater stress on the composition of shots ('mise en scène') than on their order.

But whatever he did invariably failed to impress Stalin. Stalin was, after all, a little neurotic, and he was convinced all film-makers were counter-revolutionaries. He it was who enforced a code of socialist realism that meant that all Soviet films until the collapse of Communism (with the exception of a very few, such as Tarkovsky's), were as patriotic as bread queues – and just as tedious.

Agitprop

Lenin commissioned a propaganda train to take his message around the country. Just think what he might have achieved had they had TV! The train contained a conference hall, school, library, printing press and a cinema. Films were produced by Edouard Tissé and his young editor, Dziga Vertov, and they promoted the Bolshevik cause.

ROLL THE CREDITS

It all began so well and then deteriorated. Russia's artists and intellectuals welcomed the Russian Revolution and the new government under **Lenin** *and they produced movies, plays, novels and paintings celebrating their brave new world. But by the Stalin years, they had all fallen out of favour, and* **Uncle Joe Stalin** *was not a good guy to fall out with.* **Vsevolod Meyerhold**, *with whom Eisenstein often worked in theatre, was arrested in 1939 and died in custody. Their pal, the writer* **Vladimir Mayakovsky** *shot himself in 1930 and Stalin banned his plays. Writers* **Osip Mandelstam**, **Isaac Babel** *and* **Evgeny Zamyatin** *all disappeared in Gulags and* **Mikhail Bulgakov** *was expelled from Russia. Even Stalin's censor-in-chief,* **Boris Shumyatsky**, *who planned the never-built Cine City as a Soviet Hollywood in the Crimea, was shot in 1938.*

The aftermath of the famous 'Odessa Steps' sequence from Eisenstein's classic *Battleship Potemkin* (1925).

1912 The supposedly unsinkable *SS Titanic* goes down after hitting an iceberg off Newfoundland. Several movies will be made about it, culminating in James Cameron's *Titanic*, the most expensive movie ever made, in 1998.

1914 Charlie Chaplin premieres his Little Tramp character, complete with twirling cane, bowler hat and baggy pants.

1917 Dutch-born dancer Mata Hari is convicted of having spied for the Germans and executed.

1912~1930

Shadows and Streets
German Cinema

Ask a German moviegoer of the late 1910s to name their favourite film and odds-on it would have come from either Hollywood or Scandinavia. The dark, brooding dramas directed by Danes such as Carl DREYER (1889–1968) and the Swedes Victor SJÖSTRÖM (1879–1960) and Mauritz STILLER (1883–1928) left an indelible mark on the German film psyche. Forget the glossy costume dramas of Ernst LUBITSCH (1892–1947). Shadows, symbolism and the supernatural were the truest expression of the defeated nation's post-war despair.

Maria, the robot in *Metropolis*, stirs up the workers to revolt.

Robert WIENE's *The Cabinet of Dr Caligari* (1919) set the tone. A tale of murder and madness, it used distorted sets, sinister backdrops and stylized acting to convey its narrator's tenuous grip on reality. To some it was 'painting in motion', to others it was nothing but a flagrant enticement to Hitler. Many tried to imitate it, but *Caligari* remained the one genuinely Expressionist feature.

There were certainly Expressionist elements in the work of *Fritz LANG* (1890–1976). Lang had a flair for spectacle and flitted effortlessly between crime films (*Dr Mabuse, the Gambler*, 1922, *M*. 1931), fantasy (*Die Nibelungen*, 1922–1924) and sci-fi (*Metropolis*, 1926). In Hollywood

exile from 1933, he occasionally took time off from embroidering his past to direct such classics as *Fury* (1936) and *The Big Heat* (1953).

F.W. MURNAU (1888–1931) also cut his teeth with chillers, most notably the first-ever vampire movie, *Nosferatu* (1922); but his chief claim to fame is the introduction of 'subjective camera' – the method of shooting scenes from the characters' viewpoint. In *The Last Laugh* (1924), Murnau moved the camera on bicycles, fire-engine ladders and overhead cables to suggest the movements of hotel doorman Emil Jannings, while he used superimpositions, unfocused lenses and distorting mirrors to depict his decline and fall.

1922 German architect Ludwig Mies Van der Rohe invents ribbon windows, strips of glass interspersed with concrete.

1924 The first round-the-world flight is completed in a plane made of plywood, spruce and linen canvas. The journey took 15 flying days over a period of 5 months.

1930 Rastafarians in Jamaica hail the new Ethiopian president Haile Selassie as 'the living God'.

Lights! Camera! Action!

Mounting tension.

Although the camera moved to follow the action, it was always a spectator. In *The Last Laugh* (1924), F.W. Murnau turned it into a 'character', by showing us events from the viewpoint of the onscreen characters. In addition to helping us identify with specific characters, 'subjective camera' hides facts from us and thus increases tension. Think of detective Martin Balsam climbing the stairs in *Psycho*.

Another key development was 'invisible editing'. Pioneered by G.W. Pabst, this disguised the often distracting cut to a new camera angle by waiting until a character or object was moving across the screen, so that we were too preoccupied with the action to notice the sudden shift in viewpoint. Simple, perhaps, but no one's ever found a better way to do it.

Equally innovative was 'invisible editing', which had been pioneered by *G.W. PABST* (1886–1967) in such gritty studies of urban poverty as *The Joyless Street* (1925) and *Pandora's Box* (1928). Cutting between camera angles while a character or object was in motion not only helped disguise the edit, but also made the action flow more smoothly.

Hollywood seized on both techniques. But it was soon preoccupied with another new-fangled toy – sound.

ROLL THE CREDITS

The unsung hero of the golden age of German cinema was **Erich Pommer**. *As the head of the state-owned UFA, he gave directors like Lang, Murnau and Pabst their heads and was rewarded with a string of classics. Cameraman* **Eugen Schüfftan** *also made a key contribution, as his Schüfftan Process allowed live action and models to be combined in convincing special effects. There was no shortage of actors of the calibre of* **Emil Jannings**, *but the screen goddesses were all imports.* **Asta Nielsen** *was from Denmark,* **Greta Garbo** *was Swedish and* **Louise Brooks** *was American. Greta was alone in finding sound stardom.*

Werner Krauss plays Dr Caligari, with Conrad Veidt and Lil Dagover, in front of stylized canvas sets.

Dracula's father

Bram Stoker had no idea what he was starting when he invented Count Dracula, the bloodsucking creature of the night, in 1897. The story inspired F.W. Murnau's *Nosferatu* (1922), which Stoker's widow tried to sue for breach of copyright; Bela Lugosi's 1931 *Dracula*; Francis Ford Coppola's 1992 version; and numerous other horror spin-offs, including a lesbian vampire movie, a blaxploitation vampire comedy and even a Tom Cruise vampire.

1927 Dancer Isadora Duncan is strangled to death when her long scarf becomes entangled in the wheels of a sports car.

1929 The yo-yo is introduced to the US by Donald F. Duncan.

1930 Pope Pius XI bans Catholics from using contraceptives.

1927~1935

You Ain't Heard Nothin' Yet
The Talkies

Wurlitzers provided the sound track.

How could you call them silent movies? Even the humblest fleapit had a resident pianist, while the grander dream-palaces boasted Wurlitzers and sound machines such as the Allefex. Prestige productions often came complete with scores by the biggest names in classical music. The stars had faces. Who needed to hear them talk?

Sound had been on the cards since the early 1900s. But the Hollywood moguls had always resisted its introduction. Silents had a universal appeal. Talkies meant language barriers and lost markets. They meant stars with foreign accents becoming unintelligible and those with voices at odds with their images degenerating into laughing stocks. And why break the bank wiring for sound when Talkies might be a passing fad?

But by the mid-1920s, admissions were plummeting as audiences got tired of formularized melodramas and endless caption cards. So when Warners released *The Jazz Singer* in 1927, it was an act of desperation, not triumphalism. The gamble paid off and millions flocked to see Al Jolson blurt out a few hits and the immortal line, 'Wait a minute... wait a minute. You ain't heard nothin' yet.'

Ditching the Vitaphone disc system in favour of a more reliable sound-on-film process, the studios began signing up Broadway's biggest stars. Dialogue was handcrafted by writers of the calibre of F. Scott Fitzgerald and William Faulkner, while the songs were knocked out by Tin Pan Alley's finest.

Anyone who's seen *Singin' in the Rain* knows it was a tricky transition. Performers had to huddle round microphones hidden in plant pots.

1931 The Star-Spangled Banner becomes the US national anthem.

1933 President Roosevelt broadcasts 'fireside chats' on radio, urging listeners to trust the banks and have faith in his New Deal.

1935 In Germany Heinrich Himmler introduces a state breeding programme to produce an Aryan super-race; blonde-haired, blue-eyed women are asked to volunteer to sleep with SS officers.

ROLL THE CREDITS

As well as The Jazz Singer, *Warner Bros. were to have massive hits with* Casablanca, Rebel Without a Cause *and* My Fair Lady, *and they managed the careers of* **James Cagney**, **Bette Davis** *and* **Humphrey Bogart**, *amongst others.*

Jolson Talks!

'Wait a minute, wait a minute. You ain't heard nothin' yet! Wait a minute, I tell you. You ain't heard nothin' yet! D'you want to hear "Toot, Toot, Tootsie"?'

Hardly Shakespeare, but this was the speech that made *The Jazz Singer* the most talked-about talkie. Director Alan Crosland nearly called 'cut' on Al Jolson and only an insistent Sam Warner stopped it being edited out. Sadly, Sam died before he saw his gamble pay off – big time.

The first Talkie is about a cantor's son torn between show business and the synagogue.

Noisy cameras were consigned to the 'ice box', an immobile soundproofed booth. Cross-cutting was all but prohibited by the difficulties of matching sound and vision. Was it all worth it? The subtle imagery of the silent era had been replaced by illustrated radio.

However, there were those who saw sound as something more than just a gimmick. Eisenstein enthused about its ability to extend a film's world beyond the confines of the frame, while *René CLAIR* (1898–1981) recognized its symbolic potential.

By 1930, the technical glitches had largely been ironed out and the masterpieces began to flow. Alfred Hitchcock sent shivers with screams in *Blackmail*. Lewis Milestone promoted pacifism in

All Quiet on the Western Front and Marlene Dietrich fell in love again in Josef von Sternberg's *The Blue Angel*.

Film industries flourished throughout the world. But none could hold a candle to Hollywood, which was about to enter its golden age.

Gene Kelly and Jean Hagen tell the story of the transition to sound in *Singin' in the Rain* (1952).

TINSEL TALK

Emil Jannings received the first-ever Best Actor Oscar just before he sailed home to Germany, his Hollywood career in tatters because his accent was too thick for American audiences. Vamp supreme Pola Negri also booked her passage. And while the Clara Bows and John Gilberts of this world could smoulder in silence, the moment they opened their mouths they got laughs in all the wrong places. Looks like the Broadway thesps of today are the Hollywood stars of tomorrow.

1922 In London, police commissioner William Horton is murdered with arsenic-filled chocolates.

1928 Al Jolson stars in *The Singing Fool* and becomes forever linked with the song 'Mammy'

1932 Radio City Music Hall, the world's largest cinema, opens with 5,945 seats.

1920s~1940s
The Studio System
The Majors

Who boasted more stars than there are in the heavens? Which lunatics took over the asylum? Where is Poverty Row? And whose logo was a giant aerial? No idea? What you need is a quick studio tour.

The Fox and the Lion.

Let's start at the top. Fronted by Louis B. Mayer, MGM was Hollywood's thoroughbred. No one did period pictures, melodramas or musicals with quite the same class. Its lavish productions promised glamorous, feel-good escapism for all the family and, thanks to such dependable craftsmen as George Cukor, King Vidor and Victor Fleming, it rarely failed to deliver. With an unrivalled galaxy of stars that included the King and Queen of Tinseltown – Clark Gable and Myrna Loy – MGM was an all-American success story.

There was a dash of European pizzazz about the pictures produced at Paramount. Here Josef von Sternberg composed 'poems in fur and smoke' for Marlene Dietrich, while Ernst Lubitsch made his cheekily continental comedies. As you'd expect of Cecil B. DeMille's studio, decadence and desire were the watchwords

of Adolph Zukor's relaxed regime. Yet, it was also a comic's haven, with the Marx Brothers, Mae West, W.C. Fields, Bob Hope and director Preston Sturges on the books.

Warner Bros. was a studio with its sleeves rolled up. Gritty gangster movies, social problem pictures and gutsy musicals were the staples. Pennies weren't pinched so much as throttled, as Jack, Albert and Harry tied stars of the calibre of Bogart,

Louis B. Mayer 'looks after' his protégés Mickey Rooney and Judy Garland.

1934 Bonnie and Clyde die in a hail of bullets after their 2-year crime sprees across the US catches up with them.

1941 Amy Johnson dies in a plane crash over the Thames. It later transpires that she was accidentally shot down by British forces.

1944 Paramount pays $35,000 for the mink and sequin costume Ginger Rogers wears in *Lady in the Dark*.

Busby Berkeley's extravagant choreography for movies like *Gold Diggers of 1933* astonished his audiences.

ROLL THE CREDITS

It's a hit and miss career being a screen God or Goddess. **Clark Gable** *was turned down by Zanuck because he thought he looked like an ape. And* **Myrna Loy** *might have remained an exotic vamp girl for her entire career if* **W.S. Van Dyke** *hadn't cast her opposite* **William Powell** *in* The Thin Man *and given them both some zappy dialogue. And the Oscars were the most unpredictable lottery of all. Greats like* **Barbara Stanwyck** *(who received 4 nominations) and* **Cary Grant** *(who had 2) never won at all.* **James Stewart** *won 1 from 5,* **Henry Fonda** *1 from 3,* **Gary Cooper** *2 from 5,* **Spencer Tracy** *2 from 9 and* **Katharine Hepburn** *4 from 12.*

Cagney and Bette Davis to swingeing contracts. Yet the ruthless efficiency paid off. Just look at the choreography of Busby Berkeley, the biopics of William Dieterle and the adventures of Michael Curtiz, who also made a little number along the way called *Casablanca*.

I Love Lucy.

The ultimate film factory, however, was 20th Century-Fox. Darryl F. Zanuck favoured brassy musicals, folksy nostalgia and spectacles that showed off the studio's famed SFX unit. On the payroll side: Tyrone Power, Alice Faye and Betty Grable twinkled valiantly in the shadow of Shirley Temple, while John Ford was far and away Fox's finest film-maker.

The last of the Big Five was Hollywood's youngest studio. Although home to Fred and Ginger, King Kong and Citizen Kane, and a clearing house for independents like Selznick, Goldwyn and Disney, RKO was always on its uppers. Decimated by Howard Hughes, its bleeping aerial was silenced in 1953 when it was bought by TV sitcom queen, Lucille Ball.

An enigmatic star

The MGM galaxy included the most enigmatic star of all time, Greta Garbo. Louis B. Mayer signed her in 1925 and, 27 films later, she lost faith in movies in 1941 and moved to New York, where she became a recluse. She had already weathered the death of her mentor Mauritz Stiller in 1928 and jilted the so-called love of her life John Gilbert at the altar on their wedding day. She was only 37 when she left Hollywood and never married, fuelling a plethora of scurrilous rumours that she was a lesbian and also that she was involved with photographer Cecil Beaton. However, Garbo was never tempted to spill the beans so the mysteries remain.

1925 Ancient seashells are found in the Sahara Desert, proving it was once underwater.

1933 Hitler decides that Expressionists are degenerates and many artists are persecuted and their works burned.

1940 The first McDonald's hamburger stand opens at a drive-in cinema near Pasadena.

1920s to the 1940s
The Studio System
The Minors

Things becoming any clearer? You will have noticed by now that each of the studios had a distinctive character and that lumping them together under the title 'Hollywood' scarcely does justice to their individuality and diversity. But enough of this. Let's hit the other side of the tracks.

Universal promoted Deanna Durbin as a youthful innocent.

Columbia produced *Gilda* (1946) as a vehicle for sex bomb Rita Hayworth, but David O. Selznick made *Gone With the Wind* as an independent.

A powerplayer in both the silent and blockbuster eras, Universal was a poor relation during the Golden Age. Without the legendary horror cycle and the sub-operatic warbling of teen sensation Deanna Durbin, we would never have seen the classic Basil Rathbone *Sherlock Holmes* series. But then again, we'd have been spared Abbott and Costello. Columbia also eked out a living on second features, mostly westerns and comedy series. But under the management of the much-detested Harry Cohn, it also produced the odd prestige picture, thanks to his policy of hiring stars on single-movie deals. Cohn's chief meal ticket was Frank Capra, although Howard Hawks also did some of his best work here. And when it came to the ladies, it was Rita Hayworth's name that dominated the 1940s.

Douglas Fairbanks, Mary Pickford, D.W. Griffith and Charlie Chaplin were the 'lunatics' who founded the asylum known as United Artists in 1919. Controlling your own artistic destiny was one thing, but a studio with no stars, facilities or cinemas was always going to struggle. A distribution deal with Alexander Korda hardly swelled the coffers, although a partnership with Sam Goldwyn did mean access to the stylish melodramas of William Wyler.

But the Minors lived in the lap of luxury compared to the residents of Poverty Row.

1943 Shoes are rationed. In the US, three pairs a year are allocated while in the UK, people are only allowed one pair a year.

1946 Freak blizzards sweep across Europe at harvest time destroying crops, particularly wheat.

1949 A bumper year for Ealing comedies in Britain with the release of *Passport to Pimlico, Kind Hearts and Coronets* and *Whisky Galore!*

Republic and Monogram were the aristocrats of the B-Hive, yet even they were forced to churn out programmes on insulting budgets to impossible deadlines. The diet of thick-ear actioners and hoary horse operas was only occasionally leavened by the odd surprise hit or cult classic. But many a big name director got his start in the bargain basement.

For all their airs and graces, the independents weren't always flush, either. But 1939 proved a bonanza year, with four of the ten Best Picture nominations going to indie productions – Hal Roach's *Of Mice and Men*, Walter Wanger's *Stagecoach*, Sam Goldwyn's *Wuthering Heights* and, the eventual winner, David O. Selznick's *Gone with the Wind*.

D.W. Griffith, John Barrymore, Mary Pickford, Douglas Fairbanks and Joseph M. Schenk.

ROLL THE CREDITS

Carl Laemmle *created Universal and is credited with inventing the star system, by promoting* **Florence Lawrence** *(known as the Biograph and the IMP girl) and then* **Mary Pickford.** *Laemmle was one of the few moguls whose friends outnumbered his foes.* **David O. Selznick** *drove everyone to distraction with his endless stream of memos, while* **Louis B. Mayer** *turned a blind eye to junior stars like* **Judy Garland** *being fed with slimming pills, uppers and downers, to ensure she was always bright as a button before the cameras. No one could mangle the language quite like* **Sam Goldwyn**, *who coined such gems as 'include me out' and 'a verbal contract isn't worth the paper it's written on'. But the most detested was* **Harry Cohn.** *As comic* **Red Skelton** *commented on the day of his well-attended funeral, 'Give the people what they want to see and they'll come out for it'.*

TINSEL TALK

In a town that was already famous for serial marriages, Rita Hayworth had her fair share. After the collapse of her first, to businessman Ed Judson, she became engaged to Victor Mature, Gilbert Roland, Howard Hughes, Tony Martin and David Niven before finally marrying Orson Welles in 1943. They divorced in 1948 and she married Prince Aly Khan; that marriage ended in 1953 and crooner Dick Haymes became husband number four, the most short-lived of the bunch.

1930 Clinton Eastwood Jr is born in San Franciso; he wisely drops the second syllable of his Christian name when his movie career begins in the 1960s.

1931 Al Capone is fined $80,000 and sentenced to 11 years in prison for income-tax evasion.

1937 *Snow White and the Seven Dwarfs* is released; it is the first feature-length technicolour animated film.

1930s and the 1940s

You Dirty Rat
The Great Gangsters

Paul Muni as gangster psychopath in *Scarface.*

As the major studios flourished, each developed its own signature and Warners, famously, could never get enough of crime – or, indeed, its perpetrators. From 1930 onwards, with the success of Little Caesar, *Warners became synonymous with the rattle of machine-gun fire, rapid-fire editing and rat-a-tat dialogue, as they plundered true stories of mob violence for their gritty dramas. Run with extreme frugality, Warners was a studio in touch with the Depression era, both in its modus operandi and in its film output. It embraced in sensational style such social issues as the liberties taken by the gutter press (*Five Star Final, *1931) and penal injustice (*I Am A Fugitive From A Chain Gang, *1932).*

Nonetheless, it was the gangsters who kept the tills ringing, and in Edward G. Robinson and James Cagney, Warners owned a near-franchise on fast-talking tough guys, although Paul Muni was impressively psychopathic in United Artists' *Scarface* (1932). Robinson, a man of some sophistication who grew to loathe his criminal stereotyping, made his mark as Rico Bandello in *Little Caesar* and played a string of killers throughout the 1930s before succeeding in breaking out of his casting straitjacket.

Cagney's career followed a similar trajectory, although his star shone even brighter. His breakthrough came when he famously pushed a grapefruit into Mae Clarke's face in *Public Enemy* (1931), which caused a stir commensurate with Mr Blonde's earectomy six decades later. Chafing under Jack L. Warner's financial and commercial constraints, Cagney, nevertheless, turned

Cagney never actually uttered the immortal phrase 'you dirty rat'; it just seems as if he did.

1941 The Japanese bomb Pearl Harbor, killing 2,400 Americans; 1,300 are wounded and 1,000 reported missing.

1942 The world's largest gun is used by the Germans during the siege of Sevastopol; its barrel is 95 feet long and it weighs 1,344 tons.

1945 As the German army collapses, the Reichsbank is robbed of sums of money that would be equivalent to $4 billion today.

Edward G. Robinson and Bogey in *Brother Orchid* (1940).

in some unforgettable performances for the studio, notably in *Lady Killer* (1933), which involved more domestic violence for Mae Clarke, *Angels With Dirty Faces* (1938), *Each Dawn I Die* and *The Roaring Twenties* (both 1939). Finally, Cagney proved he was more than just a mean wielder of machine guns and citrus fruits by scooping an Oscar for his portrayal of George M. Cohan in *Yankee Doodle Dandy* (1942). All the same, perhaps his most famous mob role came in 1949 as the mother-fixated Cody Jarrett in *White Heat* (1949).

It was as second banana to Cagney, Robinson and the gangster's gangster, George Raft, that Humphrey Bogart earned his spurs in Hollywood. His enduring appeal would be achieved in a darker, lonelier place.

ROLL THE CREDITS

In his first movie, Public Enemy, *Cagney was originally cast in a supporting role, but director* **William A. Wellman** *promoted him to lead during shooting.* **Paul Muni** *made his name with the lead in* **Howard Hawks'** Scarface *(1932) but his genius lay in playing historical characters like Emile Zola and Louis Pasteur.* **George Raft** *was a famously poor judge of scripts and seemingly turned down the lead in* **Billy Wilder's** Double Indemnity, *letting* **Fred MacMurray** *take the role, with* **Edward G. Robinson** *as his boss. He also turned down* The Maltese Falcon, High Sierra *and* Casablanca. *Clearly he chose roles by saying 'Heads I do it, tails I don't' on that famous coin he was always flipping.*

Bogart and Bacall

Howard Hawks inadvertently played matchmaker when he cast 18-year-old model Betty Perske as the girl who teaches Bogie to whistle in *To Have and Have Not* (1944) – 'You just put your lips together and blow'. The director was delighted at the frisson their burgeoning romance lent to the film but Bogie's wife Mayo Methot wasn't so pleased. They divorced, Bogie and Bacall married, and when he died of throat cancer in 1957, Bacall put a small gold whistle in his coffin.

Behind this second-stringer there was a movie icon just waiting to get out.

1927 Alleged spies Sacco and Vanzetti go to the electric chair amidst worldwide protests that the charges should be dropped due to lack of evidence.

1932 The world's longest recorded dance marathon ran for 4,152 ½ hours, from June 6 to Nov. 30. The prize was $1,000.

1934 Jean Vigo dies of septicaemia at the age of 29. He manages to finish directing l'Atalante but has to hand over the editing to his assistant and doesn't see the finished film.

1927~1939

Cheek to Cheek
Musicals

With impeccable bad-timing, Hollywood went music-mad just as the Jazz Age came to a close. Following Warners' experimental Lights of New York *(1928), which used sound and dialogue to great effect, billboards everywhere boasted '100% talking, 100% singing, 100% dancing' movies. Ditties found their way into everything from crime films to costume dramas. But by 1930, audiences had become so bored with the endless crooning that the same billboards were promising song-free entertainment.*

Fred and Ginger in
Swing Time, directed by
George Stevens.

Ernst Lubitsch rehabilitated the genre with witty musical comedies like *One Hour with You* (1932), but it was escapist spectacle that the punters wanted in the Depression years – and it was served up in style by *Busby BERKELEY* (1895–1976).

Buzz turned the humble musical into an art form. In 1933 alone he choreographed *42nd Street*, *Gold Diggers of 1933* and *Footlight Parade*, using kaleidoscopic and zoom lenses, audacious camera movements and rhythmic editing to fashion ludicrously extravagant numbers. Feminist critics now decry his moving sculptures of scantily clad chorus girls, but his 'top shot', gazing down on shifting geometrical patterns, is one of cinema's recognizable trademarks.

ROLL THE CREDITS

Fred Astaire *was not a one-woman man. Although he made ten films with Ginger, he also danced with a galaxy of other Hollywood beauties including his sister Adele; the Love Goddess* **Rita Hayworth** *(a cousin of Ginger's);* **Judy Garland**, *aka Dorothy in* The Wizard of Oz; **Cyd Charisse** *(whose real name was Tula Ellice Finklea); tap dancer* **Eleanor Powell** *(who later became a church minister); and the coquettish French actress* **Leslie Caron**. *After all that, a man wouldn't have the energy for much else!*

1936 The Hoover Dam is completed. Rising 726 feet above the Nevada River, it is the world's tallest dam.

1937 Two famous ballets premiered in London, Ninette de Valois's *Checkmate* and Frederick Ashton's *Les Patineurs*, forming the basis for a new style of ballet.

1939 Pepsi Cola challenge their rivals, Coke, with a new jingle: 'Twice as much for a nickel, too/Pepsi-Cola is the drink for you'.

Censorship

The Catholic League of Decency was mortally offended by the goings-on of these scurrilous movie people, on and off screen. They went to parties, got drunk, had punch-ups, slept with each other's wives and they even got divorced. What kind of role model was that for American youth? A new Production Code was imposed on the industry from 1934 that forbade certain words, gestures and actions. Films that failed to meet the Code's strict moral standards might not be distributed, or could attract hefty fines. So no more explicit violence, sexual innuendo or, the most often-quoted example, no more bedroom scenes without the man having at least one foot firmly on the floor.

LEFT Shirley was only seven years old when she starred in *The Littlest Rebel* (1935).

BELOW Betty Grable's legs made her the most famous pin-up of WWII.

'Can't act. Can't sing. Slightly bald. Can dance a little.' Yet *Fred ASTAIRE* (1899–1987) went much further than the talent scout who penned these words having viewed a screen test of the human Mickey Mouse.

With their Art Deco designs and simple stories, Fred's RKO musicals with *Ginger ROGERS* (1911–95) were ridiculously chic, but became magical the moment they began to dance. 'He gives her class and she gives him sex' was Katharine Hepburn's shrewd verdict. Had Dorothy Jordan not dropped out of *Flying Down to Rio* (1933) to get married, gems such as *Top Hat* (1935) and *Swing Time* (1936) might never have been made.

Elsewhere Jeanette MacDonald and Nelson Eddy warbled their way through the light operatic repertoire at MGM, where Judy Garland and Mickey Rooney seemed to be constantly 'puttin' on a show'. Universal stayed afloat thanks to that full-voiced Miss Fixit, Deanna Durbin, while Alice Faye and Betty Grable enlivened Fox's brand of brassy Americana. But the studio's hottest property was Shirley Temple, the tot superstar who, after 31 films and a decade of unrivalled success, became a teenage has-been.

1931 The Empire State Building is completed. It stands 1,250 feet high.

1935 Alcoholics Anonymous is founded in the US by Dr. Robert Smith and Bill Wilson.

1936 During the making of a Russian film *Little Nightingale*, 150,000 plates are shattered in the scene where women workers revolt in a porcelain factory.

1930s
Insults and Innuendo
Sharp-talking Comedy

All Charlie Chaplin needed to make a comedy was, in his words, 'a park, a policeman and a pretty girl'. For the silent era, this might have seemed minimalist, but with the coming of sound there arose from the fertile training ground of vaudeville a generation of comedians who needed no props, just their own verbal dexterity to create laughter.

The two comic greats played competing con artists in the 1940 movie.

The cruel physical humour of Laurel and Hardy found its verbal equivalent in the Marx Brothers where the only props required were an old taxi horn and the occasional pair of scissors, and absurd imperatives such as 'Go and never darken my towels again' were the norm. Led by the relentlessly caustic Groucho, the brothers were a vaudeville act who brought their anarchic routine to the screen with little embellishment. Harpo was silent, communicating only through harp solos and the toot of the aforementioned horn, Chico was his interpreter, speaking with an exaggerated Italian accent, while Zeppo was surplus to requirements and was dropped after *Duck Soup* (1933). Groucho's relentless pursuit of money and women – invariably played by his perfect foil Margaret Dumont – provided a constant theme in their films, which were never more than an extended collection of sketches but rarely less than entertaining.

Groucho is president of a banana republic and Harpo and Chico play spies in *Duck Soup*.

With similar roots in vaudeville, but an even more dyspeptic world view, *W.C. FIELDS* (1879–1946) carved himself a unique place in film history with his misanthropic comedy, which successfully crossed the divide from the silents to sound. Fields starred in over 40 features and shorts. Speaking with his inimitable nasal drawl he fashioned a screen persona based on a love of strong drink and a hatred of just about everything else.

W.C. Fields plays Mr Micawber in *David Copperfield* (1935).

1937 The Hindenburg, an airship built by the firm of Luftschiffbau Zeppelin in Germany, explodes killing 35 passengers and crew.

1938 A fish is found in the Comoro Islands that scientists thought had become extinct 75 million years ago.

1939 Italian dictator Benito Mussolini publishes his autobiography. He banned *Duck Soup* in Italy; presumably he found the satire a bit close to the bone.

Daughter of a heavyweight boxer, *Mae West* (1892–1980), another childhood vaudevillian, created a screen character which was, like Fields', larger than life, but based on a desire to make love, rather than war, with the world. Blowsy and buxom (the serviceman's lifejacket was rechristened after her pneumatic figure), West's material revolved endlessly around her sexuality and required her to employ the double entendre and sexual innuendo to get her material past the censor. Her drawled aphorisms entered the universal lexicon and her stage and screen career continued well into her ninth decade.

The final link between vaudeville and screen comedy was provided by Bud Abbott and Lou Costello, whose physical similarity to Laurel and Hardy, combined with their game stupidity, enabled them to become America's favourite double act until Lewis and Martin updated their routine. It says much for their inanity that in *Abbott And Costello Go To Mars* they land on Venus.

ROLL THE CREDITS

MGM's golden boy **Irving Thalberg** *(on whom Scott Fitzgerald's novel* The Last Tycoon, *filmed by Scorsese and De Niro in 1976 was supposedly based) successfully poached the Marx Brothers from Paramount. Thalberg reined in much of their anarchic comedy, saddling them with juvenile leads whose romance and warbling wasted much screen time, as did Harpo's harp solo and Chico's piano slot. There used to be a fifth Marx brother,* **Gummo**, *who was dropped from the act before they reached Broadway in the late 1920's.* **Zeppo** *went on to be a talent agent, with Barbara Stanwyck, Clark Gable and Carole Lombard amongst his clients.*

In their own words

MAE WEST: "Is that a gun in your pocket or are you just pleased to see me?" "Whenever I'm caught between two evils, I take the one I've never tried." "When women go wrong, men go right after them."

GROUCHO MARX: "A man is only as old as the woman he feels." "Whoever named it necking was a poor judge of anatomy." "Please accept my resignation. I don't want to belong to any club that would have me as a member."

W.C. FIELDS: "Anyone who hates children and dogs can't be all bad." "I am free of all prejudice. I hate everyone equally." And his reason for not drinking water – "Fish f*** in it."

Cary Grant and Mae West spar in *She Done Him Wrong* (1933).

1931 Two German students are the first to conquer the north face of the Matterhorn.

1933 It is the height of the American Depression when *King Kong* is released but it is still a remarkable commercial success. Its star, an 18-inch model, is created by Willis O'Brien.

1934 Mens' undershirt sales plummet after the release of *It Happened One Night*, because Gable doesn't wear one in the film.

1930s and 1940s
200 Words a Minute
Screwball Comedy

The changes that overtook Hollywood in the decade following the release of The Jazz Singer *(1927) constituted nothing less than a revolution, unequalled except for the first 10 years of cinema's existence.*

Claudette Colbert and Clark Gable.

Hepburn and Grant star alongside a leopard called Baby.

Compare, if you will, the flickering image and crackling sound of Al Jolson's voice with the clarity of the photography and crisp dialogue of, say, Bringing Up Baby *(1938) released only 11 years later. Such a pace of change brought with it inevitable casualties, notably the silent stars with the squeaky voices and, as public taste grew more 'sophisticated', slapstick comedy fell on its own banana skin.*

In truth, however, slapstick didn't so much die as become reborn in the guise of screwball comedy, which enjoyed its heyday as a genre in the 1930s and 1940s. The characteristics of screwball comedies were rapid-fire, wisecracking dialogue; a relentlessly paced plot; no shortage of visual gags and situations where sane people behaved insanely (thereby harking back strongly to ancient notions of comedy as an inversion of the world order). Executed by some of Hollywood's greatest directors, it proved a winning formula.

Howard Hawks, a master of so many genres, turned in three classic screwballs with *Twentieth Century* (1934), *Bringing Up Baby* and *His Girl Friday* (1940), the latter two both with Cary Grant; but it was Sicilian immigrant Frank Capra who became the master of this American genre.

Capra catered to the needs of the Depression nation with a series of feelgood films that saw the small man prevail often in the face of selfishness and corruption – *Mr Deeds Goes To Town* (1936), *Mr Smith Goes To Washington* (1939) and *Meet John*

1935 Shirley Temple becomes the number one box-office star at the age of seven.

1943 Swiss chemist Albert Hofmann accidentally discovers the halucinogenic effects of LSD while experimenting in his lab.

1947 Pilot Kenneth Arnold sees nine circular objects in the sky, like "saucers skipping over the water", and the term "flying saucer" is invented.

Doe (1941) – although the film for which he is best remembered today, *It's A Wonderful Life* (1946), flopped on its release to a more cynical post-war audience. It was Preston Sturges who brought a more baleful vision to the genre in the 1940s with films like *Sullivan's Travels* (1941) that mocked much of Capra's wide-eyed idealism.

In a similar screwball vein but with a stronger populist appeal, Bob Hope, Bing Crosby and Dorothy Lamour starred in seven 'Road' movies beginning with 1940's *Road To Singapore*. Fast-paced and with contemporary, knockabout humour, the 'Road' series established its stars as among America's most beloved entertainers. But the rapid change in public taste, mirrored so frequently in the frantic speed of screwball comedy, dictated that no act could hope to remain popular indefinitely. The American public, as brutal as any audition agent, shouted 'Next!'.

ROLL THE CREDITS

Cary Grant *had wooed and won most Hollywood stars by the time he retired at the age of 61, on screen at least. Off screen, he married five times, his wives including actresses* **Virginia Cherrill, Betsy Drake, Dyan Cannon** *and Woolworth's heiress* **Barbara Hutton.** *He also had a clandestine affair with cowboy star* **Randolph Scott.** **Katharine Hepburn,** *Grant's co-star in* Bringing Up Baby, *had a long-standing personal and professional relationship with* **Spencer Tracy.** *They met making* Woman of the Year *(1942) and starred in a string of comedies together, including* Adam's Rib *(1949) and* Pat and Mike *(1952). He never divorced his first wife, Louise Treadwell, but it was Hepburn that nursed him through the last years of his life.*

Jack of all trades

While most directors in the studio era specialized in a particular genre or type of film, Howard Hawks tried them all. As well as screwball comedy, he directed a gangster movie (*Scarface*, 1932), a war film (*The Dawn Patrol*, 1930), westerns (*Red River*, 1948 and *Rio Bravo*, 1958), film noir (*The Big Sleep*, 1946), a prison picture (*The Criminal Code*, 1930), action adventures (*The Crowd Roars*, 1932), a melodrama (*Only Angels Have Wings*, 1939), a musical (*Gentlemen Prefer Blondes*, 1953) and even sci-fi (*The Thing from Another World*, 1951 – whIch he clearly directed despite Christian Nyby getting the credit).

The famous screen partnership of Tracy and Hepburn produced many gems, including Pat and Mike.

1930 The winner of the International Cocktail Competition is the Golden Dawn, made of gin, apricot brandy, Calvados, orange juice and grenadine.

1937 Edward VIII abdicates the throne of Great Britain so that he can marry his American lover, Wallis Simpson.

1939 Carmen Miranda starts a trend for wearing fruit on your head.

1930s and the 1940s
Why Ask for the Moon?
Women's Pictures

From the earliest years of the century women had made up more than half of the cinema-going population, but the formula thought up for liberating them from their money wouldn't have involved 50 per cent of the average halfwit's grey matter. A woman's choice was simple: she could either swoon over the latest matinee idol or weep over the romantic journey of an empathetic female such as Gloria Swanson.

Paul Henreid lights two cigarettes in *Now Voyager*.

With the coming of sound the sisterhood set their hearts on suffering in a big way and the two stars who vied with each other for martyrdom dominated the women's picture for the next two decades: *Bette DAVIS* (1908–1989) and *Joan CRAWFORD* (1904–1977).

Famous for their long-running and much-hyped feud – Davis once said of Crawford: 'The most fun I had with her was pushing her downstairs in Baby Jane' – the couple actually had much in common. Neither was conventional, film-star good-looking (Universal tycoon, Carl Laemmle, once remarked unchivalrously of Davis: 'I can't imagine any guy giving her a tumble'), but both had an indomitable will to succeed. And both had unflattering memoirs written about them by their daughters.

Davis' determination saw her go on strike at Warners in a demand for better material (she lost the case, but won the argument), and by 1938 she was a double

Oscar-winner and about to enter her most successful era: this included, in 1942, one of the defining weepies, *Now Voyager*, which saw her transformed by Paul Henreid's doomed love. A slump in her popularity in the late 1940s was countered by her magnificently bitchy performance in *All About Eve* (1950), and she remained active in film until her death.

Bette and Joan play sisters in *What Ever Happened to Baby Jane?*

1943 Howard Hughes designs a cantilevered bra to fit Jane Russell's 38-inch bust. She later confesses it was unwearable.

1947 Dior launches the 'New Look' a romantic style of dress design, with long skirts, petticoats, unpadded shoulders, narrowed waists, and padded hips.

1951 The first Miss World contest takes place and is won by Miss Sweden.

'Fiddle-de-dee!' Scarlett flounces outside Tara, the ancestral home in *Gone With the Wind*.

ROLL THE CREDITS

The public taste for weepies is apparent from the Best Actress Oscar nominations in 1938: **Greta Garbo** *for* Camille *(woman dying of consumption);* **Barbara Stanwyck** *for* Stella Dallas *(woman gives up daughter to rich family where she will have a better life); and* **Janet Gaynor** *for* A Star is Born *(woman gets more famous than her partner and he becomes an alcoholic).* **Luise Rainer**, *nominated for her role as a suffering Chinese peasant in* The Good Earth, *didn't think she stood a chance against that competition and hadn't turned up for the ceremony. They had to phone her at home and ask her to dash downtown straight away when she won.*

Crawford was similarly tough and redefined herself with each passing decade. Written off as 'box-office poison' in 1945, she took the lead in *Mildred Pierce* (a part rejected by Davis and Barbara Stanwyck) and took Oscar glory as the long-suffering heroine. She moved from victim to villain in the post-war era, although retreated into familiar suffering territory for her successful pairing with Davis in *Baby Jane* (1962).

Hollywood liked romantic couples in their women's films, particularly if the pair in question were an item off screen as well. Thus, Spencer Tracy and Katharine Hepburn were one of the most successful pairings from *Woman of the Year* (1942) onwards, while Bogart and Bacall smouldered their way through *To Have And Have Not* (1945). Hollywood couldn't deliver the moon, but the stars, at least, were no problem.

Rhett and Scarlett

Based on Margaret Mitchell's Pulitzer-prize-winning novel, *Gone With the Wind* was a massive success as soon as it opened. Clark Gable was everyone's choice for Rhett Butler. But Hollywood's finest actresses had to fight it out for the part of that headstrong Southern belle Scarlett O'Hara. Bette Davis and Katharine Hepburn had fallen by the wayside and Paulette Goddard looked set to star, until Tinseltown was rocked to its foundations when an English actress, Vivien Leigh, pipped her at the post. Producer David O. Selznick went through four directors – George Cukor, Sam Wood and Victor Fleming amongst them – and fifteen screenwriters, including F. Scott Fitzgerald. For the great fire scene, 30 acres of abandoned sets were burned and the total cost was remarkable for its day at over $4 million.

1933 The 21st Amendment finally ends Prohibition in the US, bringing an end to bootlegging, speakeasies and rum-running.

1942 The Allies arrive in Casablanca and liberate the city two days before the release of the film.

1955 Nabokov's controversial novel *Lolita* is published; the 1962 film starring James Mason raised the girl's age to 14 to make it more acceptable to audiences.

1910s to the present
Home on the Range
Westerns

Never has Hollywood revealed its power to rewrite history more completely than with the western. As America sought a national identity and a sense of cohesion, the western provided the country with a rose-tinted view of its roots which extolled pioneering values and the irrefutable logic that the men in the white hats always won. The bloody business of colonization and genocide wasn't addressed; it wasn't until Broken Arrow *in 1950 that Hollywood produced a talkie that saw events from the perspective of the Native American. As America interrogated its past, so the western retreated from unquestioning supremacy to moral ambiguity and thence to near extinction.*

John Wayne in
Stagecoach.

Cheap to make with readily available locations, westerns were a staple of silent cinema, but the godfather of the genre in the era of sound was *John* FORD (1895–1973). Here was a craftsman whose confidence in his ability – he edited with his camera, shooting a minimum of extra footage – was echoed in his bold and powerfully realized films; *Stagecoach* (1939), *My Darling Clementine* (1946), *The Searchers* (1956) were three definitive examples. *Howard* HAWKS (1896–1977) cut down on the sentiment and brought an added realism to *Red River* (1948) and *Rio Bravo* (1959).

ROLL THE CREDITS

Raoul Walsh *worked on ranches breaking horses before going into the movie business in 1909, so it was no surprise that he gravitated towards westerns, such as* They Died with Their Boots On *(1942), about Custer. Walsh lost an eye when a rabbit crashed through the windscreen of the jeep he was driving while making* In Old Arizona *(1929).*

Italian director **Sergio Leone** *created the so-called spaghetti western with* A Fistful of Dollars *(1964) followed by* For a Few Dollars More *(1965) and* The Good, the Bad and the Ugly *(1966). These made* **Clint Eastwood** *a star in the role of* The Man With No Name *while his 1992 success in* Unforgiven *proved the genre is by no means moribund.*

1962 Marilyn Monroe sings Happy Birthday Mr President to John F. Kennedy.

1969 On 20 July at 10.56.20 Eastern Time, Neil Armstrong plants his left foot on the surface of the Moon.

1972 Peter Bogdanovich's movie *What's Up Doc?* is based on *Bringing Up Baby*.

Kim Darby and John Wayne star in *True Grit* (1969). Wayne got an Oscar for his role as the boozy lawman.

The western genre enjoyed an unrivalled period of popularity that lasted until the 1950s. Along with such marque directors as Ford and Hawks, however, the genre also churned out countless support features, unremarkable yet popular, and several stars were born. There was Tom Mix, the prototype for the all-action western hero, William Boyd – aka Hopalong Cassidy – and singing cowboys, Gene Autry and Roy Rogers. Then there was John Wayne.

Dances with Wolves

Kevin Costner's directorial debut was officially approved by the Sioux it portrays, but other Native Americans complained that all the characters were stereotyped as stoical, brave and ecologically aware. The film is overlong and sentimental – perfect Oscar fodder in other words. It received twelve nominations and seven awards, including Best Film and Best Direction, proving that the industry at least still isn't tired of tales of the pioneering spirit. Many of Costner's other movies, including *Robin Hood: Prince of Thieves* (1991) and *Waterworld* (1995) feature him as the lone hero in a hostile environment where, invariably, a man still has to do what a man has to do.

Gary Cooper and newcomer Grace Kelly play man and wife in Fred Zinneman's *High Noon* (1952).

Picked from B-Movie obscurity by John Ford to star as the Ringo Kid in *Stagecoach*, Wayne became one of Hollywood's best-loved stars and a national institution. His stolid acting style was mirrored in the tough no-nonsense characters he portrayed on screen.

As the appeal of the western faded in the late 1940s, the genre reinvented itself with more thoughtful fare and intelligent allegories. *High Noon* restricted its action to the final reel, focusing on Gary Cooper's psychological ordeal, while *Bad Day At Black Rock* (1955) took a classic western formula and translated it into a modern-day setting.

1929 In the St Valentine's Day Massacre Al Capone's gunmen, dressed as policemen, execute seven members of the 'Bugs' Moran gang.

1931 The world land speed record is broken by Malcolm Campbell at Daytona Sands, at a speed of 245 miles per hour.

1939 Einstein writes to President Roosevelt urging him to develop the atomic bomb before Germany does.

1920s to the present

The Swashbucklers
Early Action Heroes

In a nation where the tendency towards the huge is evident in everything from burgers to buttocks, it's no surprise that Hollywood has always cherished its big men. Beef on the bone has never been banned in the US and today's musclebound action heroes can trace their lineage back to the swashbucklers of the 1920s and 1930s.

Foremost amongst these handsome heroes were *Douglas* FAIRBANKS (1883–1939) and *Errol* FLYNN (1909–1959). The former, one-time husband of 'America's Sweetheart' Mary Pickford and co-founder of United Artists, cut a dash as Zorro, Robin Hood and D'Artagnan before handing the crown to Flynn. The dashing Tasmanian defined the devil-may-care insouciance – without which no card-carrying swashbuckler could prosper – in *The Adventures Of Robin Hood* (brilliantly parodied by Danny Kaye in *The Court Jester*) among many others, before achieving notoriety when charged with statutory rape of two teenage girls. His hard living destroyed his good looks and career and cut short his life in 1959.

Flynn, it was said, had wearied of his heroic typecasting, a trap which *Burt* LANCASTER (1913–94) skilfully avoided. He made his name in such top-off fare as *The Crimson Pirate* (1952) and *Trapeze*

Errol Flynn demonstrates his expert sword play in *Sea Hawk* (1940), directed by Michael Curtiz.

(1956), but always looked to alternate these parts with more substantial drama such as *From Here To Eternity* (1953) and *Sweet Smell Of Success* (1957).

Clearly seeking to imitate the career path of Lancaster was *Kirk* DOUGLAS (1916–), a muscular leading man who might usefully be regarded as the progenitor of the modern action hero, given his unstinting appetite for naked combat as seen in *Spartacus* and *The Vikings*. Douglas similarly looked for more than beefcake roles, however, and in *Ace In The Hole* (1951) as a cynical newsman and *Lust For Life* (1956) as Vincent Van Gogh he proved himself superior to all his leaden latter-day imitators.

1958 The Campaign for Nuclear Disarmament (CND) is founded in the UK.

1966 John Lennon claims that the Beatles are more popular than Jesus Christ.

1970 Frank Sinatra appears before a Commission of Inquiry into Organised Crime and denies any links with the Mafia.

The missing link (in more ways than one) between these reluctant beefcake stars of the 1950s and 1960s and Schwarzenegger and Stallone came in the square-jawed and frequently loincloth-clad figure of *Charlton HESTON* (1924–   ). Cast as the hero of innumerable epics, Heston has been Ben-Hur, El Cid, Moses and Michelangelo. His stiff acting style nevertheless achieved Oscar recognition (for *Ben-Hur*), but in recent years he has become best known for his anti-liberal, pro-guns crusade (he famously fought for the suppression of rapper Ice-T's *Cop Killer* album). He found a new generation of fans, however, when he starred in *Planet Of The Apes* (1968). To utter the line 'Take your stinking paws off me, you damn dirty ape', without breaking into laughter is surely the mark of some sort of genius.

ROLL THE CREDITS

What was a hero without a vile villain to joust with? **Basil Rathbone** *will forever be Sherlock Holmes. But as Guy of Gisbourne in* The Adventures of Robin Hood *(1938), he thrust and parried his way through the screen's longest swordfight with* **Errol Flynn**. *There were occasional swashbucklettes too.* **Jean Peters** *turned pirate in* Anne of the Indies *(1951), although her most famous role was as Mrs Howard Hughes.*

Ben-Hur
The making of the movie nearly bankrupted MGM. Director William Wyler, who had worked as assistant director on the 1925 silent version, used more than 8,000 extras in some scenes and the set covered more than 18 acres, making it one of the biggest in cinema history. The chariot race between Ben-Hur and Messala, which lasts 20 minutes on screen, actually took 3 months to shoot at the Cinecittà studios in Rome. The total cost was $15 million but this was easily earned back and at the following year's Oscars it took Best Picture, Best Director, Best Actor and 8 other awards, equalled only by *Titanic* in 1998.

Charlton Heston in *Ben-Hur*'s famous chariot scene.

1923 Edwin Hubble discovers that the universe contains other galaxies and is much bigger than previously thought.

1927 *Metropolis* costs a record 5 million marks and takes 11 months to film, despite the fact that they use miniatures instead of building the huge sets originally planned.

1931 Ella Wendel of New York leaves $20 million to her poodle, Toby, making him the world's richest dog.

1920s~1948

Hollywood Horror
Vampires, Monsters and a Giant Ape

The 1930s was a time of misery and ruin for many ordinary Americans. The Great Depression had wiped out the stock market and unemployment was running at an all-time high. Yet in 1931, long cinema queues were waiting to see Bela Lugosi as Dracula. As in Germany in the 1920s, the national plight had translated itself into an appetite for the fictional horrors of the big screen.

The 1931 hit was based on a play by Peggy Webling and Mary Shelley's novel.

Bela Lugosi feasts on Helen Chandler in his classic 1931 *Dracula*.

The key figure in the invention of the modern horror movie was the director Tod Browning. During the 1920s he was best known for his silent collaborations with Lon Chaney (the 'Man of a Thousand Faces'), who specialized in excruciating contortions and grotesque make-up best exhibited in *The Hunchback Of Notre Dame* (1923). Browning originally wanted Chaney to play Dracula in Universal's film, but instead chose Bela Lugosi. Although the star of the stage play, Lugosi was completely unknown, and thus cheap. The movie was a hit despite a slew of objections from censorship boards across the country, and Lugosi so identified with the role that when he died in 1956 he was buried in his Dracula cape. Browning went on to direct the infamous *Freaks* in 1932 (a Gothic melodrama with a cast of real 'freaks'), Universal moved full-speed ahead to bring to life that other Gothic horror, Frankenstein's monster (with the British director James Whale). Lugosi turned the part down, disappointed by the lack of dialogue, and a virtual unknown, Boris Karloff, landed the role.

By now, the horror cycle was in full swing. *Bride Of Frankenstein* (1935) and

1933 A London surgeon takes the first photograph of the Loch Ness monster.

1944 London is bombarded with doodlebugs.

1947 Thor Heyerdahl crosses the Pacific on a raft called the *Kon-Tiki*. It takes 101 days and he doesn't meet anyone on the way across.

Quasimodo looks for his Esmerelda.

Transformation

Lon Chaney, known as the 'Man of a Thousand Faces', grew up with deaf-mute parents with whom he communicated by mime, thus developing his acting skills from an early age. The hideous make-up that he designed and applied himself created a sensation in roles such as 'Frog' in *The Miracle Man* (1919) and Quasimodo in *The Hunchback of Notre Dame* (1923). For the latter, he used 70 pounds of padding to create the famous hump. As the grotesquely disfigured composer in *Phantom of the Opera* (1925), he designed a device that spread his nostrils wide and pulled back his lips to reveal protruding teeth. Celluloid disks padded his cheeks and a domed wig with straggly bits of hair covered his head.

Dracula's Daughter (1936) would eventually capitalize on the success of their progenitors while new characters made their first appearances.

The audience's thirst for terrifying movies was seemingly unquenchable, even if censors opposed the making of such films (particularly in puritanical Britain, where many were banned) and horrified critics looked desperately for a reason for this sudden darkening of America's tastes.

But, by the end of the decade, the public's appetite for the latest monstrosity from Hollywood was almost sated; there was another and much more real horror just around the corner.

After the Second World War, the great Universal monsters would either vanish or be reduced to comedy cameos such as *Abbott and Costello Meet Frankenstein* (1948).

ROLL THE CREDITS

Merian C. Cooper *and* **Ernest B. Schoedsack** *met in Poland during the First World War and began working together as directors of documentary-style features such as* Grass *(1925) about the lives of Persian nomads, and* Chang *(1927), set in China. Their interest in anthropology and adventure meant it was not a complete change of course when they made their most famous film in 1933,* King Kong. *The star was created by SFX wizard* **Willis O'Brien**, *who animated six 18-inch models made of a metal frame covered with sponge rubber and rabbit fur. Close-ups of the monster were filmed using a giant bust operated by three men inside it.*

King Kong is brought to New York where he captures Fay Wray and creates havoc.

1928 Bubble gum is invented by a 23-year-old accountant called Walter Diener. Dubble Bubble is the first brand he markets.

1952 German unicyclist Rudy Horn sets a world record when he throws six cups and saucers with his feet and balances them on his head while riding a unicycle. He then adds a teaspoon and a lump of sugar.

1956 A.A. Milne, the creator of Winnie the Pooh, dies.

1928~1998
The Kingdom of the Mouse
Birth of the Cartoon

Animation – where do you begin? With the delightful pre-camera films of Émile Reynaud? Or those silent superstars Gertie the Dinosaur, Felix the Cat, Betty Boop and Popeye the Sailor? What about the abstract animations of Viking Eggeling and Oskar Fischinger? What indeed? Or the puppet films of Wladyslaw Starewicz, Jiri Trnka and Jan Svankmajer? No, best keep it simple, and start with a mouse who originally rejoiced under the name of Mortimer.

Betty Boop provided the love interest in the early cartoon world.

Lights! Camera! Action!

Cartoons are created by a laborious technique called stop-frame cinematography. The camera films a series of drawings, or frames, that differ only minutely from each other so that when they are played in sequence at the normal rate of 24 frames per second, they give the illusion of movement. Rather than completely redraw the scenes every time, animators covered the background with transparencies called cels on which the characters were painted, so that only the moving figures had to be redrawn for each frame. Nowadays computer technology is used and it's difficult to tell which bits are animation and which are special effects.

The first animated feature, it took four years to make and cost $1.5 million.

When *Walt DISNEY* (1901–1966) and his partner *Ub IWERKS* (1900–1971) released Mickey Mouse's debut cartoon, *Plane Crazy*, in 1928, animation was cinema's poor relation. Requiring some 14,400 individual drawings for a ten-minute cartoon, it was a time-consuming way to plug the gaps between the main feature, the B-Movie and the newsreel.

1963 Tippi Hedren is attacked by life-size mechanical birds and has some real ones attached to her clothing in Hitchcock's famous movie.

1965 3-dimensional holograms are possible using laser technology.

1982 The catch phrase 'ET phone home' was heard everywhere after the release of Steven Spielberg's extra-terrestrial movie.

ROLL THE CREDITS

Hollywood can't claim all the credit here! Lots of international film-makers contributed to the development of cartoons. The first animated cartoons were produced before 1910 by pioneers such as Frenchman **Emile Cohl** *and American* **Winsor McCay** *(his film* Sinking of the Lusitania *in 1918 is claimed to be the first animated feature). German animator* **Lotte Reiniger** *employed mobile silhouettes; fellow Germans* **Oskar Fischinger** *and* **Viking Eggeling** *and New Zealander* **Len Lye** *experimented with abstract designs choreographed to music; and* **George Pal** *of Holland refined the techniques for puppet animation. Since 1940, Canadian animator* **Norman McLaren** *and the National Film Board of Canada have been influential in inventing new techniques and finding new uses for the old.*

of America (UPA) in 1941, pipping their former boss to Oscars with films featuring Mr Magoo and Gerald McBoing-Boing.

Back in Hollywood's golden age, the major studios also had their own animation departments. The most inspired was based at Warners, where artists of the calibre of Tex Avery, Friz Freleng and Chuck Jones devised such characters as Bugs Bunny, Daffy Duck and Porky Pig. Still, MGM did all right with Joseph Hanna and William Barbera, the creators of Tom and Jerry, who would come into their own when cartoons found a new home on TV, with *Yogi Bear*, *The Flintstones* and *Top Cat*.

Disney's dominance of animation has become even stronger and *Beauty and the Beast* (1991) became the first cartoon to be nominated for a Best Picture Oscar. Warners can compete on a merchandizing basis and now, Steven Spielberg's DreamWorks enters the fray.

Ub Iwerks drew the first Mickey Mouse in 1928.

But Disney changed all that. *Snow White and the Seven Dwarfs* (1937) confounded the critics and laid the foundation for the billion-dollar empire that now boasts theme parks, media conglomerates, an ice-hockey team and even its own town.

There were hiccups along the way as the competition mounted. A number of animators quit to form United Productions

He speaks!
In the first Disney sound cartoon, *Steamboat Willy* (1928), it was Walt himself who provided the squeaky voice of Mickey Mouse.

1910 *Howard's End*, by E.M. Forster, is published. The movie version 83 years later earns a Best Actress Oscar for Emma Thompson.

1929 Penicillin is used for the first time by Alexander Fleming in a London hospital. He washes an assistant's sinuses in a penicillin broth, curing their infection.

1944 D Day. A huge fleet crosses the English Channel to win Europe back from the clutches of Hitler.

1910s to 1950s

Cliffhangers and Crimebusters

Series and Serials

Following a proud literary tradition, the film serial came into being with Edison's What Happened to Mary? *in 1912. However, it was the sight of Pearl White surviving* The Perils of Pauline *(1914) that turned audiences into serial addicts, haunted all week by the latest cliffhanger ending and those all-too-familiar words, 'to be continued' – agonizing!*

Although the popular image is that of a plucky heroine strapped to the railway tracks by a moustache-twirling villain, the serial was soon the stamping-ground of the action hero. Some, such as Dick Tracy and the Green Hornet, solved their first cases on the radio, while Batman, Captain Marvel and Superman sprang from the pages of comic books. Others, including Flash Gordon and Buck Rogers, confounded dastards in outer space, while the Red Ryder and the Lone Ranger righted wrongs out west.

The undisputed king of the serials was 'Buster' Crabbe, although Kane Richmond, Tom Tyler and Don 'Red' Barry pushed him close. Kay Aldridge and Linda Stirling were the pick of the best gals, while George B. Seitz, Spencer Gordon Bennet and William Witney wielded the meanest megaphones.

The serial bowed out with *Blazing the Overland Trail* in 1956. But as long as 007 has a licence to kill, the movie series looks

Buster Crabbe was the most famous of the serial action heroes.

set to survive and the 1990s have seen revivals of characters like Dick Tracy and The Shadow. Surprisingly, MGM was the home of the series: with Tarzan, Dr Kildare, Maisie and the irrepressible Andy Hardy all based there. Columbia weighed in with Blondie and Jungle Jim, while Universal gave the world Ma and Pa Kettle and Francis, the Talking Mule.

The Poverty Row studios specialized in Wild West series like *The Three Mesquiteers*, *The Cisco Kid* and William Boyd's Hopalong Cassidy adventures. They also made a unique contribution to the series picture with the introduction of such cultural icons as singing cowboys Roy Rogers, Gene Autry and Tex Ritter.

Serialization

As marketing ideas go, it's an oldie but a goodie. Get your audience hooked and then stop right at crisis point so they have to pay for the next issue to see what happens. Charles Dickens was doing it back in the 1830s when *Oliver Twist* ran in monthly instalments in a magazine called *Bentley's*. From 1919, radio dramas were broken into instalments to entice the audience to tune in again. Usually the stories tell of innocent victims against the forces of evil, with perhaps a comic sidekick helping them. There are frequent climaxes and confrontations to raise the emotional tension. And, of course, it all led up to the bête noire of modern society, the soap opera.

Vivacious Pearl White always survived the perils encountered by Pauline, to come back in the next episode.

Crime, however, was the true B-series staple. The Bowery Boys had their share of scrapes with the law, but it was sleuths such as Sherlock Holmes, Charlie Chan and Mr Moto and troubleshooters like the Saint, the Falcon and the Lone Wolf who were the real crowd-pleasers. Pacey, improbable and impenetrable, their cases remain compelling viewing 60 years on.

Roy Rogers rides Trigger, the most famous horse in the West.

ROLL THE CREDITS

Pearl White *was the first serial superstar, although she spent most of* The Perils of Pauline *tied to railway tracks, hanging from crumbling ledges or screaming silently from the back of runaway cars. Over 100 Tarzan movies have been made since* **Elmo Lincoln** *first donned the loincloth in 1918. But the busiest screen character is Sherlock Holmes, who has solved more than 210 cases since 1900, with* **Basil Rathbone** *being the most popular resident of 221B Baker Street. As Andy Hardy,* **Mickey Rooney** *launched the cult of the American teenager, albeit of the clean-cut variety.*

1937 The Golden Gate Bridge is completed in San Francisco. It is the longest bridge in the world, at 4,200 feet.

1947 William Randolph Hearst leaves his famous San Simeon mansion (portrayed as Xanadu in *Citizen Kane*) and retires to Beverly Hills with his mistress Marion Davies.

1959-62 D.H. Lawrence's novel *Lady Chatterley's Lover* is censored and its publishers prosecuted for obscenity in Britain, Canada and the US, more than forty years after its first publication.

1927~1971

Murder and MacGuffins
The Master of Suspense

Choose motels. Choose Mount Rushmore. Choose bell towers. Choose a seaside town with a large, psychotic avian population. Choose answering your phone while Anthony Dawson waits behind you in the dark with a big pair of scissors. Choose death.

"It could be the most terrifying motion picture I have ever made!"

STARRING
ROD TAYLOR   JESS
A UNIVERSAL-INTERNATIONAL RELEASE   Screenplay by EVAN HUNTER · Directed by A

The Award Winning   INCIDE

The Birds contains 371 trick shots, including the spectacular pull away from a blazing garage.

Cameos

Having stood in as an extra on *The Lodger*, Hitch made a point of cameoing in his pictures. In *Blackmail* he's pestered by a kid on the tube, while in *Strangers on a Train* he boards with a cello case. In *Lifeboat* he appears in a newspaper ad, while in *Dial M for Murder* he's in a reunion photo. He narrated the prologue to *The Wrong Man* and was a mere silhouette in *Family Plot*. But his triumph was *Under Capricorn*, in which he popped up twice.

For five decades, no matter what the venue, no matter how innocent matters may have appeared, *Alfred* HITCHCOCK (1899–1980) always delivered the goods – invariably dead on arrival. The most famous director of the century, his portly profile and adenoidal wheeze were known to millions thanks to his famed cameo appearances and his

two TV series: *Alfred Hitchcock Presents* and *The Alfred Hitchcock Hour*.

Hitch began his career as a pioneer of British silent cinema with a Jack-the-Ripper-inspired yarn, *The Lodger* (1927), and directed one of the first British talkies, *Blackmail* (1929). An early thriller *The 39 Steps* (1935) introduced his recurrent theme of the wrong man caught up in danger. He moved to the US and won an Oscar nomination for *Rebecca* (1940), but remarkably no Academy Awards ever came his way. His most acclaimed sequence

1963 The film *RoGoPaG* creates a scandal in Italy for undermining state religion. It's name comes from the four directors involved: Rossellini, Godard, Pasolini and Gregoretti. Welles played a director making a religious epic.

1965 The worst power failure in history blacks out seven states on 9 November. Phone services are retained and New Yorkers make a record 62 million calls in one day.

1967 Muhammad Ali is banned from boxing for three and a half years for refusing to fight in the Vietnam War.

PLEASE DO NOT SEE THE END FIRST!!!
See it from the beginning:

ALFRED HITCHCOCK'S
The Birds"
TECHNICOLOR   **X** CERT

e Du Maurier's classic suspense story!

· SUZANNE PLESHETTE
and Introducing 'TIPPI' HEDREN

OWL CREEK Ⓐ

What Makes A Good Film?

Despite the dubious honour of being one of the most recognizable and written-about directors of all time, Hitch retained a bluff realism about the worth of his work. He himself considered *Shadow of a Doubt* (1943) – in which Joseph Cotten plays a murderer who goes to stay with his unwitting relatives – his best American film. 'A good film,' he once declared, 'is when the price of admission, the dinner and the babysitter was well worth it.' Few can argue with that.

came between 1954 and 1960, when he reeled off such classics as *Rear Window*, *Vertigo*, *North By Northwest* and *Psycho*: a run of films which saw the director alternating between experimental offerings and box-office paydirt. His later years saw no lessening of his capacity to shock, with *Frenzy* (1972) earning an 'R' certificate for its strangulation scene.

Hitchcock's films – stylish, menacing and, arguably, misogynistic – have received the ultimate accolade: becoming a genre in their own right.

Grace Kelly and James Stewart watch out for a murderer in *Rear Window* (1954).

1930 The Communist party newspaper *The Daily Worker* is launched in London. It will continue to appear until 1941.

1934 Italy wins the World Cup with a 2-1 victory over Czechoslovakia in Rome's Stadio Torino.

1935 The board game Monopoly is invented by Charles Darrow. The object is for players to attempt to bankrupt each other.

1930s

Flatcaps and Fantasy
Britain in the 30s

Entering the 1930s, the British film industry found itself in a uniquely healthy position, as the snappily-titled Kinematograph Film Act of 1927 had successfully limited the number of foreign films that could be shown in the country and stimulated the industry at home dramatically. The decade would see the production of some of the most prestigious, successful British films ever made and the flourishing of homegrown talent on the big screen. But by its end, Britain's brief, presumptuous attempt to take on Hollywood was all over. Yet it would be unfair to blame all of this on George Formby.

George Formby was instantly recognizable for his buck teeth and ukulele.

Hollywood's reaction to the Depression was an invigorating mix of down-to-earth gangster pictures, lavish musicals and romantic escapism. Britain sought to tackle those no-job, means-tested, Jarrow Marching blues with a combination of George Formby, Gracie Fields and Will Hay: possibly in a paternalistic attempt to alleviate Northern unemployment.

'Our Gracie' entertained the boys at the Front but never became famous in the States.

Their appeal lost much in translation and they made no inroads in America, but on this side of the Atlantic they ruled the box-office. *FORMBY* (1904–1961), a buck-toothed Lancastrian who clutched his ukulele to his chest almost as tightly as he did his native stupidity, was supremely popular from 1936 onwards, while comedienne and singer *Gracie FIELDS*

Quota Quickies
According to the terms of the Kinematograph Film Acts of 1927, 27% of all films shown on British screens had to be homemade. Although it was supposed to boost national cinema, the 'Quota Act' had the opposite effect. Rather than risk money on more prestigious projects, producers churned out dozens of so-called 'quota quickies', B-Movies made on a pittance at breakneck speed that satisfied the folk at the quota office and no one else. Although the golden age of the quickie was the 1930s the term was used as dismissive shorthand for any low-budget British movie right up to the early 1960s.

1936 Billy Butlin opens the first Butlins holiday camp at Skegness two hours from London. It accommodates 1,000 guests but space has to be doubled within a year due to demand.

1938 Daphne du Maurier writes *Rebecca*. Hitchcock films this plus two other works by her – *Jamaica Inn* and *The Birds*.

1939 Britain rations meat, cheese, fats and sugar and consumption of milk, potatoes and green vegetables goes up.

(1898–1979) had no pre-war British female rival. *Will Hay* (1888–1949) successfully transferred his music-hall talent on to the big screen, but his film career stalled in the early 1940s.

More significantly perhaps, in 1931, after fleeing his native Hungary and leading a nomadic existence across Europe and America, *Alexander Korda* (1893–1956) finally settled in Britain. There he founded London Films and turned his substantial experience to producing and directing a sequence of popular and critically acclaimed films: notably *The Private Life of Henry VIII* (1933) starring the peerless Charles Laughton, *Things to Come* (1936) and *The*

ROLL THE CREDITS

Despite his hooded eyes, bushy brows and bald head, one of **Alistair Sim's** *most famous roles was in drag, as the headmistress in* The Belles of St Trinian's *(1954). Fresh-faced* **John Mills** *excelled in character roles such as Pip in* Great Expectations *(1946) and the title role in* Scott of the Antarctic *(1948). Wide-eyed, bucktoothed* **Jessie Matthews** *was best in musicals like* The Good Companions *(1933).* **Margaret Lockwood** *began life as a plucky heroine in films like Hitchcock's* The Lady Vanishes *(1938). But fame came as a scheming beauty in period penny dreadfuls like* The Wicked Lady *(1945), produced by Balcon's Gainsborough Pictures.*

A film produced by Alexander, directed by Zoltan and designed by Vincent Korda.

Goodbye Mr Chips (1939). But by the time the latter was released, a combination of mounting debt and fear of an uncertain future had fatally undermined British film's brief resurgence and triggered a number of studio bankruptcies. Serious competition to Hollywood had died in its infancy and for the big battalions of the American film industry, it had turned out nice again.

Four Feathers (1939). Meanwhile *Michael Balcon* (1896–1977), co-founder of Gainsborough Pictures, took over at Gaumont British and then MGM British. He oversaw such quintessentially British films as *The 39 Steps* (1935) and

Charles Laughton plays the corpulent monarch in *The Private Life of Henry VIII* (1933).

1926 Sculptor Constantin Brancusi fights and wins a court case to decide whether *Bird in Space* is a work of art and therefore exempt from the 40% import duty customs are trying to charge him.	**1937** The town of Guernica is destroyed by General Franco's troops aided by German bombers. A famous painting by Picasso commemorates the event.	**1945** Mussolini is shot and Hitler commits suicide.

1920s~1998
Talking Heads and Flies on Walls
Documentary Cinema

Night Mail,
express delivery.

Representations of reality? Life was hard enough without the cinema ramming its realities down your throat. Consequently, once the novelty of the Lumières' actualités had worn off, the non-fiction film became something of a cinematic backwater. Newsreels accompanied most screenings, but few punters were willing to pay good money specifically to see documentaries – even masterworks like Robert Flaherty's Nanook of the North *(1922) or Walter Ruttmann's* Berlin, Symphony of a Great City *(1927).*

Sound transformed the documentary. Commentaries and interviews not only made them seem more relevant, but also gave them a cutting edge, particularly in the hands of such persuasive political film-makers as the Dutchman, Joris Ivens, and the American, Pare Lorentz.

Yet during the 1930s, it was the British Documentary Movement that was the envy of the world. Presided over by John Grierson (who first coined the term 'documentary'), the members of the GPO Film Unit deftly combined poetry and polemic in deceptively powerful films that included Basil Wright's *Song of Ceylon* (1934) and *Night Mail* (1936).

Having done its bit during the Second World War, the documentary found itself in the doldrums again in the 1950s. Television had usurped its news-gathering function, while Cold War clampdowns

Best known as a producer, John Grierson directed only one film, *Drifters* (1929).

1950-54 Senator Joe McCarthy spreads a wave of anti-Communist hysteria, wild accusations and blacklists that ruins the careers of many and causes Chaplin to relocate to Switzerland.

1961 Lady Diana Spencer, the future Princess of Wales, is born.

1997 The Spice Girls' album *Spice* reaches number 1 in 14 countries and sells 12 million copies in 6 months, making it the fastest-selling album ever by a British act.

Nanook of the North follows the daily life of an Eskimo family.

What's your point of view?

When watching a documentary, consider who is filming it, and why. And what is the attitude of those being filmed? The 'fly-on-the-wall' technique tries to convince viewers that they are seeing the protagonists in normal circumstances, sitting round a kitchen table or discussing events in the street, as though they were unaware they were being filmed. In fact, there was a film crew watching and they probably stopped frequently for takes. Would they have behaved in the same way If there were no witnesses? What do you think?

was used on Drew Associates' *Primary* (1960), Frederick Wiseman's *Titicut Follies* (1967) and the Maysles brothers' *Salesman* (1969). But the very process of footage selection for the completed film diminished any real objectivity. Nowadays anything goes as far as style is concerned – after all, subject matter is what hooks the viewer.

prevented documentarists tackling anything more controversial than art studies, travelogues and corporate promos. But with lighter cameras, magnetic sound tape and a shift in social attitudes, the genre came bouncing back in the 1960s.

In declaring that his *Chronicle of a Summer* (1961) was an 'experiment in filming the truth', Jean Rouch opened up a veritable can of cinematic worms. It came closer to depicting the everyday than a fictional film. But was it 'cinéma vérité' if Rouch was behind the camera calling the shots and on the screen setting the agenda? Chris Marker's *Le Joli Mai* (1963) was another slice of life that revealed more about its maker than its subjects.

American adherents of Direct Cinema also found it impossible to avoid personal imprints. The fly-on-the-wall approach

ROLL THE CREDITS

Making his name with studies of a bridge and a rainy day, Dutchman **Joris Ivens** *(1898–1989) shot films on all five continents. A devotee of montage, he covered conflicts in Spain, China and Vietnam, as well as the Second World War. Invariably putting a Marxist slant on things, he became the world's oldest director when he completed* The Wind *(1988) at the ripe old age of 89.*

1919 The pogo stick is invented and inspires a dance routine in the Ziegfeld Follies.

1922 T.S. Eliot publishes *The Waste Land*, expressing the disillusion of the post-First World War generation.

1929 The first Popeye cartoon appears, complete with corncob pipe, love of spinach and his girlfriend Olive Oyl.

1919~1939

Impressions and Depressions
French Poetic Realism

The charismatic Jean Gabin.

1914. Four years of war will follow and Hollywood will become the world's film capital. The story of French cinematic domination is about to fade to black. Fin.

But while the French mainstream was on its knees, the avant-garde was just beginning to find its feet. Cine clubs celebrating the 'Seventh Art' sprang up everywhere, while theorists spouted aesthetics in the growing number of film journals.

Gosh!
Jean Renoir was the son of Pierre Auguste Renoir (1841–1919), the Impressionist painter who did all those nice ballet dancers and Parisians socializing in cafés.

The leading *cinéaste* was *Louis* DELLUC (1890–1924), who wanted films to reproduce the lyricism of Baudelaire's poetry and the subtlety of the Impressionists. The combination of realism, symbolism and camera trickery demonstrated in *Fever* (1921) was emulated by disciples like Germaine Dulac (*The Seashell and the Clergyman*, 1927), Jean Epstein (*The Fall of the House of Usher*, 1928) and Marcel L'Herbier (*L'Argent*, 1929) while *René* CLAIR (1898–1981) tickled the public fancy with comedies like *An Italian Straw Hat* (1927).

'The French Griffith', *Abel* GANCE (1889–1981), was the only director linked to the avant-garde to enjoy much commercial success. *La Roue* (1922) stunned the film world with its audacity, but *Napoleon* (1927) has proved a more lasting memorial.

Mercifully free from studio or state control, film-makers combined the lyricism of the silent era with everyday realism and literate scripts to kickstart the sleeping French cinema. Recalling the Surrealists in *Zéro de Conduite* (1933)

Albert Dieudonné plays Napoleon in Gance's classic film.

1931 Peas are the first vegetables to be frozen successfully.

1933 Fatty Arbuckle dies broke and forgotten twelve years after he was tried and acquitted of manslaughter when an actress died at one of his parties.

1939 Pall Mall cigarettes launch a brand that is 15mm longer than any other and they claim that the extra length makes the smoke milder.

Cannes

The Cannes Film Festival was supposed to start in September 1939 but international events got in the way so it had to be postponed till October 1946. In his inaugural speech the new French minister of Commerce declared that 'the first Festival of Agriculture' was open. Nevertheless, it was a great success with the Grand Prix going to a French film, Jean Delannoy's *La Symphonie Pastorale*, and the best actor award to Ray Milland for his portrayal of an alcoholic in Billy Wilder's *Lost Weekend*. As far as we know, there were none of the starlets in fur bikinis, press feeding frenzies and outrageous yacht-board toga parties for which the festival is infamous today.

and Impressionism in *L'Atalante* (1934), Jean VIGO (1905–1934) fashioned the style that became known as Poetic Realism.

The prospect of peace was reflected in such optimistic features as Marcel Pagnol's *Marius* trilogy (1931–1936), Clair's *A Nous la Liberté* (1932) and Jacques Feyder's *Carnival in Flanders* (1935). Yet the fall of the Popular Front government saw films like Julien Duvivier's *Pépé le Moko* (1937) take on a darker tone. The doyen of pessimistic realism was Marcel CARNÉ (1909–1996), whose studies of doomed humanity, *Quai des Brumes* (1938) and *Le Jour se lève* (1939), both starred that barometer of French self-esteem, Jean GABIN (1904–1976). It was Jean RENOIR (1894–1979), however, who most successfully combined cinema with social commentary. He shared the nation's hopes in *The Crime of Monsieur Lange* (1936) and reflected its growing fear of fascism in *La Grande Illusion* (1937).

LA RÈGLE DU JEU

In this 1939 masterpiece, Renoir warned Europe that it was 'dancing on a volcano'. It soon erupted.

ROLL THE CREDITS

Kevin Brownlow *is the man without whom we would never have heard of Abel Gance. He came across* Napoleon *in an archive and painstakingly restored it, starting a trend for rediscovering the gems of silent cinema.*

Surrealist poet **Jacques Prévert** *wrote dark but influential screenplays which were directed by his brother Pierre (*L'Affaire est dans le Sac*), Renoir (*The Crime of Monsieur Lange*) and Carné (*Les Enfants du Paradis*).*

Equally admired was **Charles Spaak,** *for his collaborations with* **Jacques Feyder** *and* **Julien Duvivier.** *Another key factor in the impact made by the poetic realists were the meticulous sets designed by* **Lazare Meerson** *and* **Alexandre Trauner.**

1914 On December 14th German troops leave their trenches singing Christmas carols and engage in a football match with the enemy. Hostilities resume the next day.

1919 Nancy Astor becomes Britain's first woman MP.

1921 Famine kills more than 3 million Russians and frozen corpses are piled high in the streets.

1914~1945

Look, Listen, Learn

Propaganda and War

Moving pictures were first used as a weapon of war in 1898, when J. Stuart Blackton faked scenes from the Spanish-American war on a New York rooftop. Films boosted recruitment and morale on both sides during First World War, with pacifist tracts like Thomas Ince's Civilization *(1916) drowned out by such jingoistic tubthumpers as* The Beast of Berlin *(1917).*

Hitler commissioned Riefenstahl (below) to make *The Triumph of Will* at the Nazi party rally at Nuremberg in 1934.

While the documentary came of age during the war, the propaganda picture had to wait until the 1930s before it acquired any degree of sophistication.

It was *Leni* RIEFENSTAHL (1902–) who first recognized that spectacle was more likely to impress viewers than mere politicking. *The Triumph of the Will* (1935), her record of the 1934 Nuremberg rally, and *Olympia* (1938), an account of the 1936 Berlin Games, were masterpieces of PR. Yet for all their artistic merit, the films have been denounced for their messianic portrayal of Hitler. However, they were nothing compared to such invidious pictures as Veit Harlan's notoriously anti-semitic drama, *Jew Süss* (1940).

No one's suggesting that the other side played fair with its wartime propaganda. The Allies were cool and Hitler a fool in films such as Chaplin's *The Great Dictator* (1940) and *Der Fuehrer's Face* (1943), featuring the unique talents of Mr Donald Duck.

Newsreels such as *The March of Time* and *Pathé Gazette* kept people informed of the latest developments, while the British Ministry of Information and the American Office of War Information churned out shorts on everything from war bonds and munitions to careless talk and coughs and sneezes. There were films of justification – Frank Capra's *Why We Fight* series

1926 Harry Houdini makes headlines by remaining underwater for 91 minutes.

1942 The world's worst submarine disaster occurs when an American freighter rams a French submarine carrying 130 men in the Caribbean.

1945 The fire-bombing of Dresden causes more civilian casualties than the atomic bomb dropped on Hiroshima.

ROLL THE CREDITS

Josef Goebbels, the Nazi Minister of Information and Propaganda, decided to 'purify' German cultural life by favouring the artists who would produce flattering pictures of Hitler's regime. The result was a mass exodus of talent, especially by those who also happened to be Jewish. Directors **Fritz Lang, Erich Pommer, Max Ophuls** *and* **Robert Wiene** *were among the first to go; performers* **Elisabeth Bergner, Peter Lorre** *and* **Conrad Veidt** *joined in and so did cameramen* **Karl Freund** *and* **Billy Wilder.** *Yet Goebbels was a shrewd enough propagandist to know that subtly insinuating entertainments had more chance of getting the message across than Sieg Heiling fanaticism.*

(1942–1944), encouragement – Humphrey Jennings' *Listen to Britain* (1942), and patriotism – Marcel Carné's *Les Enfants du Paradis* (1945).

Directors such as John Ford, William Wyler and John Huston shot films at the front, while several stars signed up, including Clark Gable and James Stewart. Those who remained saw action in the Hollywood Canteen (a club for visiting service personnel) or in the endless round of combat adventures, home-front melodramas and escapist flagwavers.

Film would never again play such a key role in a conflict, while the war inevitably left an indelible mark on cinema.

Noel Coward and crew keep their upper lips stiff aboard *HMS Kelly* in David Lean's *In Which We Serve* (1942).

The war effort

As well as appearing in propaganda movies, various stars flew out to the front lines in Europe or the Malaysian peninsula to raise morale amongst the boys. Sex Goddess Rita Hayworth, Sweater Girl Lana Turner and Betty 'Million Dollar Legs' Grable always went down well. Bette Davis started the Hollywood Canteen, where off-duty soldiers could pop in and see stars doing cabaret turns as well as serving behind the bar and selling dances. Carole Lombard was tragically killed flying back from a tour to raise war bonds, soon after starring in the anti-Nazi satire *To Be or Not To Be.*

1942 Barbra Streisand, Harrison Ford and Martin Scorsese are born.

1943 Duke Ellington produces Black, Brown and Beige.

1944 The US navy stations six blimps off Morocco to detect submarines trying to enter the Straits of Gibraltar.

1942~1952
A Slice of Life
Neo-Realism

Rome, Open City centred around the German Occupation just six months after the end of the war.

'The ideal film,' said screenwriter Cesare Zavattini, 'would be 90 minutes in the life of a man to whom nothing happens.' A tad extreme, perhaps. But many film-makers, who had witnessed the horrors of the Second World War, had also reached the conclusion that empty escapism had had its day. Life and all its imperfections in grainy black-and-white. That was the key to one of the most influential film movements of them all – Neo-Realism.

Although inspired by Soviet cinema and French Poetic Realism, Neo-Realism was most firmly rooted in the poverty and pessimism of conflict-torn Italy. Luchino Visconti's *Ossessione* (1942) is usually deemed the earliest example, but it was Roberto Rossellini's war trilogy that fashioned the authentic Neo-Realist style. Shot in available light with a restless camera and played by largely non-professional casts improvising their lines, *Rome, Open City* (1945), *Paisà* (1946) and *Germany, Year Zero* (1947) had a raw power that sent shockwaves throughout the film world.

Strictly speaking, there's no such thing as an authentic Neo-Realist film. Even Zavattini, who was one of the movement's founding fathers, discovered feature films had to be about something. Indeed, the documentary realism in his collaborations with director Vittorio De Sica was invariably sugared with melodramatic sentimentality. Nevertheless, *Shoeshine* (1946), *Bicycle Thieves* (1948) and

TINSEL TALK

50 years on, it's difficult to understand the public outrage that followed the revelation that the 'happily married' Ingrid Bergman was pregnant by Roberto Rossellini. Moral groups fumed, a senator called her degenerate and proclaimed 'We must protect ourselves against such scourges'. In his fury, Bergman's ex-husband Dr Peter Lindstrom kept her away from their daughter Pia for eight years. The seven films Bergman made with her new spouse were coolly received. But she won back some sympathy when Rossellini dumped her for an Indian scriptwriter, leaving her to raise their son and twin daughters (one of whom is actress Isabella Rossellini) alone.

1947 Sir Thomas Beecham founds the Royal Philharmonic Orchestra and is credited with starting a Mozart craze in Britain.

1950 Gloria Swanson triumphs as fading movie star Norma Desmond in *Sunset Boulevard*, after Mary Pickford and Mae West turn the part down.

1952 The first Holiday Inn is opened on Highway 70 near Memphis. Every motel in the chain has a swimming pool and there's air conditioning and a TV set in every room.

ROLL THE CREDITS

Neo-Realism was a training ground that gave a foot in the industry to much of the talent that was to appear in Italian movies for generations. **Antonioni's** *first job was as a film critic on the Neo-Realist magazine* Black and White, *edited by Mussolini's son Vittorio.* **Fellini** *started as a script writer.* **De Sica** *was a matinée idol, the handsomest star in Italy, and he horrified the public when he turned to directing.* **Visconti** *was briefly a Neo-Realist before he turned to glossy and operatic movies such as* The Damned, The Leopard *and* Death in Venice. *And* **Guiseppe De Santis** *was accused of corrupting Neo-Realism with his young star's titillating scenes in a rice field wearing tight wet clothing.*

politically motivated pictures, and virtually outlawed Neo-Realism with a package of business disincentives in 1949.

An inspiration to and a curse on Italian cinema ever since, Neo-Realism had an incalculable impact on film-making worldwide. It proved to smaller industries that significant films could be made cheaply using local stories, talent and settings. Interestingly, it was Hollywood that most readily took these lessons to heart.

Cinecittà

One of Mussolini's more useful acts was to found the Cinecittà studio, making Rome one of the most important centres for film-making for decades. Hollywood producers filmed several big-budget movies there, including the infamous *Cleopatra*, because it worked out cheaper than filming at home. Cinecittà was bombed during the war and that is why *Rome, Open City* and *Bicycle Thieves* had to be filmed outdoors. In fact, the gritty look of *Rome, Open City* is explained by the fact that Rossellini had run out of film stock so he was buying up normal photographic film and painstakingly glueing it all together each evening ready for the next day's filming!

Silvana Mangano premiered in *Bitter Rice* at the age of 19.

Umberto D (1952) are shining examples of mise en scène technique at the service of affecting human dramas.

Just about every serious director made their Neo-Realist statement. Yet for all their international acclaim, these films were coolly received in Italy. Only the prospect of Silvana Mangano in tight shorts in Giuseppe De Santis' *Bitter Rice* (1948) created much excitement. Audiences were much more interested in catching the Hollywood movies they'd been denied during the war. The Italian government wasn't too pleased, either, with the negative image presented in these

1942 Soap is rationed in Great Britain.

1942 Italian physicist Enrico Fermi produces the first sustained nuclear reaction at the University of Chicago.

1944 *Gone With the Wind* is the first film to be shown in Paris after the Liberation.

1940s
Watch the Lady
Film Noir

Everyone's smoking: the curtains have been replaced by venetian blinds, 'dames' are forever double-crossing and nobody's thought to pay the electricity bill. Ah, that'll be the 'film noir' then. Easy to characterize and even easier to satirize, film noir was a dominating influence on American movies in the post-war era, but if its trappings appear clichéd to modern audiences; its inspiration was every bit as dark as the alleys in which all those cigarettes were smoked. A new cynicism took hold of America in the wake of the Second World War as GIs, changed by combat, returned to the country and the population faced up to the stark reality of the atomic age. This is what film noir reflected.

Barbara Stanwyck leads Fred MacMurray astray in *Double Indemnity*.

In the immediate aftermath of the Second World War, Hollywood produced a spate of so-called 'problem pictures', and the ugly topics of anti-Semitism, racism and corruption were given serious consideration in films like *Crossfire* (1947), *Home Of The Brave* and *All The King's Men* (both 1949) respectively.

A similar, new trend was that of the crime films that used real-life events as their basis. The success of pictures like *The House On 92nd Street* (1945) paved the way for films that used a grittier style of

TINSEL TALK

Lana Turner's life resembled a complex film noir. She was married eight times, twice to the same man (she said she found men 'terribly exciting'). In 1958, her 14-year-old daughter Cheryl Crane stabbed her mother's mobster boyfriend Johnny Stompanato to death. Cheryl claimed that Johnny had been sexually abusing her and beating up her mother and that she had acted in self-defence. The jury acquitted her.

1946 Legendary curmudgeon, comic and alcoholic W.C.Fields dies on Christmas Day.

1947 The Hollywood Ten are blacklisted after appearing as unfriendly witnesses in front of the House Committee on UnAmerican activities.

1949 Rita Hayworth marries Aly Khan, one of the richest men in the world, in Vallauris, France, and the whole town turns out to watch.

ROLL THE CREDITS

Philip Marlowe, Sam Spade and Mike Hammer were the hard-boiled, cool as ice detectives created by **Chandler, Hammett** *and* **Spillane**. *Yet successive directors have had very different ideas as to what makes a screen shamus. Marlowe, for example, has been played by actors as different as* **Bogart, Dick Powell, Robert Montgomery, Robert Mitchum** *and* **Elliot Gould**.

Alan Ladd *played a loner in Hammett's* The Glass Key *(1942). He was teamed with* **Veronica Lake** *again in* The Blue Dahlia *(1946), which Chandler adapted for the screen from his own story. The Lake Look – a sweep of blonde hair falling across her eyes – was recreated by* **Kim Basinger** *in* LA Confidential *(1997), a latterday noir that proved even colour films could be pitch black.*

Jack Nicholson protects wealthy widow Faye Dunaway in *Chinatown*.

ways of German Expressionism (Wilder, Preminger, Lang) and a dark, brooding anti-hero (Bogart, Mitchum, Fred MacMurray). *The Maltese Falcon* (1941) is generally regarded as the first film noir, but *Double Indemnity* (1944) is a far more cynical and shocking example of the genre.

Film noir's influence was profound and suggested that Hollywood had found a more mature way of facing up to reality (or a clever way of attracting its audience). Its influence is palpable in recent film-making: see *Chinatown* (1974), and *LA Confidential* (1997). Critics seem to be particularly fond of it as a genre, but then they do spend their lives largely in dark and lonely places.

Ridley Scott's *Blade Runner* (1982) uses the expressionist grammar of the noir genre; its femme fatale is a replicant. Or is she?

photography and employed non-professional actors and real locations, in the fashion of Italian Neo-Realism.

Thus the scene was set for the emergence of film noir. The essential ingredients were a literary pedigree (preferably an adaptation from the hard-boiled fiction of Dashiel Hammett, Raymond Chandler or James M. Cain); an alluring, but duplicitous 'femme fatale' (Barbara Stanwyck, Lana Turner, Veronica Lake); a European émigré director schooled in the

1945 The world's smallest dog, a matchbox-sized Yorkshire terrier, dies at the age of two.

1947 The term 'Cold War' is first used to describe the strategic political struggles between the US and Europe on one side and the Communist bloc on the other.

1948 Mahatma Gandhi is assassinated by a Hindu extremist.

1945~1954

The Dream is Over
Hollywood in Crisis

Immediately after the war, things couldn't have looked rosier for Hollywood. The major studios had transformed themselves into factories producing high-quality entertainment that was demanded the world over. In 1946 the industry broke all records with box-office receipts of $1.75 billion. Who could have guessed that only a year later, what had been the ultimate dream factory would be plunged into a nightmare of paranoia, suspicion, and worst of all, falling profits?

Edward G. Robinson, here seen in *Little Caesar* (1931), one of the Hollywood greats blacklisted by HUAC.

Two events would conspire to throw a spanner in the works of the Hollywood money machine. Firstly, a union strike in 1945 had forced salaries up. Then foreign countries, the UK in particular, levied massive taxes (up to 75 per cent) upon imported Hollywood films. To cap it all came the final

Dalton Trumbo and John Howard Lawson before going to start their jail sentences for having Communist sympathies.

calamity: an anti-monopoly suit, called the Paramount Decrees, which forced the studios to sell their exhibition circuits. Thus the monolithic studio system was dealt a severe blow: no longer could they make, distribute *and* exhibit their movies.

But there was even worse to come. The Cold War had generated an air of hysterical fear that America was being secretly attacked by spies and fellow travellers indistinguishable from the ordinary man in the street. In Washington, Senator Joseph McCarthy capitalized on the mood by hijacking the House of UnAmerican Activities Committee and launching a full-scale witchhunt, convinced that Tinseltown was full of Commies and 'unpatriotic elements'. 41 witnesses were called. Some – Louis B. Mayer and Walt Disney among them –

1950 The US Academy of Science warns men that there is no cure for baldness.

1952 The premiere occurs of Beckett's *Waiting for Godot*, the absurdist drama about time and eternity, alienation and loneliness, the impossiblity of true communication between people.

1954 France loses its colonial empire of Indo-China after the battle of Dien Bien Phu.

High Noon

Having appeared as a friendly witness in 1947, Gary Cooper starred in Fred Zinneman's *High Noon* (1952), an anti-HUAC western about sticking to one's principles in the midst of fear. Director Elia Kazan also testified in 1952, admitting membership of the Communist Party and naming 15 'fellow travellers'. He had earlier refused to 'name names', but claimed his change of heart was due to a realization of the dangers of Communism. His 1954 feature, *On the Waterfront*, starring Marlon Brando, was a clear allegory of his experiences. It says much for the climate in 1950s Hollywood that both won the Oscar for Best Picture.

eagerly co-operated with these shameful proceedings, naming those they imagined had Communist sympathies. Others refused to co-operate, for which crime the 'Hollywood Ten' ended up in jail, and a blacklist was drawn up of actors, writers and directors whom the studios had to ban from employment. Of these, some managed to find work in Europe, but for others – amongst them, Hollywood's finest – it meant the end of their careers, and for some,

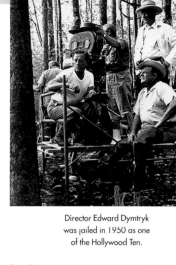

Director Edward Dymtryk was jailed in 1950 as one of the Hollywood Ten.

even their lives. It remains the darkest period in American film history, and bitterness about it lingers to this day. While the industry reeled from the shock, yet another threat was slowly opening its one flickering eye in living rooms across America. The arrival of television was about to make things even worse.

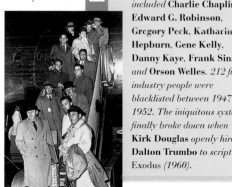

Thirteen witnesses fly back to Los Angeles in 1947, claiming 'We are returning to an industry that is still free'.

ROLL THE CREDITS

If they had jailed everyone suspected of Communist sympathies, there wouldn't have been a film industry left. In 1949 a confidential list was published of several hundred people alleged to have Bolshevik connections, and it included **Charlie Chaplin, Edward G. Robinson, Gregory Peck, Katharine Hepburn, Gene Kelly, Danny Kaye, Frank Sinatra** *and* **Orson Welles.** *212 film industry people were blacklisted between 1947 and 1952. The iniquitous system finally broke down when* **Kirk Douglas** *openly hired* **Dalton Trumbo** *to script* Exodus *(1960).*

1950 Ginetta Gloria La Bianca is the youngest singer to take an adult role in an opera when she sings the part of Gilda in Verdi's *Rigoletto* aged fifteen.

1951 Ferdinand Porsche, who had designed the Volkswagen Beetle for the Nazis, creates the first Porsche sports car.

1955 Rock Hudson marries Phyllis Gates, his agent's secretary, to prevent the public finding out he is homosexual.

1950~Present
Bigger and Better?
Gimmicks and Gadgetry

Couch potatoes; Hollywood's greatest fear.

For Hollywood executives in the 1950s, television was the ultimate nightmare. Why would people go out to the movies when they had their own free mini-cinemas in the corner of the living-room? By 1951 there were 10 million TV sets in the US, audiences were dwindling and something had to be done. The answer was a slew of gimmicks.

ROLL THE CREDITS

*If any director personified the mania for gimmicks in the 50s, **William Castle** was that man. Producing mainly ultra-low budget horror, he drew in audiences with scams like insuring them against death by fright (Macabre, 1958), wiring some of the seats with buzzers to deliver shocks at tense moments in the film (The Tingler, 1959) and pioneering 'Emergo', a 3-D system which involved a plastic skeleton being hoisted over the audience on a pulley while delighted patrons usually launched popcorn at it. Castle went on to produce the horror classic Rosemary's Baby (1968) while **John Goodman's** character in **Joe Dante's** Matinée (1993) is loosely based on him.*

How the West Was Won features a Native American attack on an express train.

The first tactic that the studios used was to convert rapidly to colour film stock. Although colour had been available since the silent era, expense had limited its use. But who could resist full-colour images when all their TVs could manage was flickering black and white?

The next move was to make the screen bigger. Cinerama, a process which entailed linking three cameras together to film a huge area, proved costly and unwieldy. Moreover, to show features like *How The West Was Won* (1962) on a screen twice as tall and three times as wide as normal required a trio of projectors, and few cinemas could afford the refit.

1956 Flat-top haircuts are fashionable.

1958 Britain's first parking meters come into operation in the prestigious London district of Mayfair.

1959 Fidel Castro overthrows Battista and takes power in Cuba.

Ray Milland in *Dial M for Murder*, which also starred Grace Kelly.

CinemaScope provided a cheaper and more convenient alternative. Based on a system that was devised for First World War periscopes, CinemaScope was an anamorphic process that required only a single camera and standard stock to optically squash the image into a frame during filming and a basic projector to unsqueeze it on the screen. There were teething problems following *The Robe* (1953), as directors worked out what to do with all that extra screen space. But widescreen soon became the norm, and modern versions were enhanced by the development of stereo sound.

More eccentric ways of interesting the audiences included 3–D, which made its mainstream debut in the jungle adventure, *Bwana Devil*, in 1952. The process, called 'Natural Vision', used two cameras filming the same scene from slightly different angles. The two images were then projected separately and viewed through polarized glasses, resulting in a 3-D image. By 1954 it was possible to project from a single film strip, but just as the technology was perfected, the public passion for it began to wane.

Although over 60 'depthies' (including Hitchcock's *Dial M For Murder*, 1954) were made in a couple of years, there were only so many rolling boulders, flaming arrows and stampeding beasts that an audience could take. Yet the gimmick value of 3-D never completely lost its appeal, and it occasionally resurfaced in films like *Jaws 3-D* (1983).

Lights! Camera! Action!
Film stock comes in all shapes and sizes. At the amateur end of the scale comes 8mm, with 16mm acting as a handy format for film school students and the cash-strapped. The majority of features are still shot on 35mm, although the IMAX widescreen system uses 65mm and the occasional spectacular like *Lawrence of Arabia* requires 70mm. CinemaScope cornered the widescreen market for most of the 1950s, although Paramount operated its own VistaVision process and producer Mike Todd pioneered the 70mm system Todd-AO.

Jaws 3-D. This time the terror doesn't stop at the edge of the water...

1954 Reverend Sun Myung Moon establishes the Unification Church. His disciples are known as Moonies.

1955 Donald Campbell breaks the world water speed record in Bluebird, with speeds of 202mph. Twelve years later he dies attempting to break his own record.

1967 Famous satirist Dorothy Parker dies; amongst her many often-quoted aphorisms, she said that men don't make passes at girls who wear glasses and that if all the girls at the Yale prom were laid end to end, she wouldn't be at all surprised.

1950s to the present
Method amidst the Madness
Playing Mean and Moody

By the early 1950s advances in cinema technology had ensured that the moving image now bore little resemblance to the early projections of the Lumière brothers half a century earlier. Yet the style of acting would not have been unfamiliar to theatregoers from the turn of the century – it was classical screen acting, heavily influenced by the traditions of English theatre. Those changes in technology, notably the coming of sound and the increased mobility of cameras, had brought greater realism and intimacy to the screen, but it was a revolution fomented in Russia which gave modern cinema acting its new – and distinctively American – voice.

The Wild One (1953) made Brando an overnight hero for rebellious youth.

Elia Kazan directs Kirk Douglas and Faye Dunaway in *The Arrangement* (1969).

Method acting as it became known traced its origins to the Russian actor, Constantin Stanislavsky who, in 1912, set up the First Studio at the Moscow Art Theatre. Looking for greater realism from actors, he taught his students to immerse themselves psychologically and imaginatively in their roles in pursuit of authenticity rather than mere mimicry. The creed was disseminated in Hollywood principally through the work of Lee Strasberg, who, along with Elia Kazan and Cheryl Crawford, ran the Actors' Studio in New York.

Marlon BRANDO (1924–) was the very embodiment of Method acting as Hollywood understood it. His screen presence in his breakthrough performance

1969 A spectator is killed by the Hell's Angels gang hired to protect the Rolling Stones at a concert in Altamont, California.

1972 Sixteen survivors of a plane crash in the Andes eat six of their fellow travellers to help them stay alive until they are rescued.

1980 Millions of people worldwide wait with bated breath to find out who shot JR in *Dallas*.

as Stanley Kowalski in *A Streetcar Named Desire* (1951) suggested a dark, rebellious sexuality combined with a cavalier disregard for personal hygiene. Hollywood found him and his naturalistic style irresistible and he won four successive Oscar nominations, culminating with an Academy Award in *On The Waterfront* (1954). His subsequent career has taken in towering success and dismal failure, controversy and catastrophe, culminating in multi-million dollar pay-packets for minimal screen cameos. But he has never been anything less than watchable.

The only pretender to Brando's Method crown was *James Dean* (1931–55), whose teen spirit was established in three films –

Rebel Without A Cause, *East Of Eden* and *Giant* – before reaching new heights of deification following his untimely death. He was posthumously nominated for Oscars for both *East of Eden* and *Giant* and his

Dean was signed to Warner Bros. after being spotted playing an Arab pederast in Gide's *The Immoralist* on Broadway.

ROLL THE CREDITS

The films of **Elia Kazan** *received 60 Oscar nominations, and he personally won Best Director for Gentleman's Agreement and On the Waterfront (see page 69). His protégés included* **Brando**, **James Dean** *and* **Warren Beatty**. **Nicholas Ray** *cast Dean in* Rebel Without a Cause, *released posthumously after Dean crashed his Porsche Spyder and died aged 24. Ray frequently directed films about loners fighting society, working with* **Bogart**, **Robert Mitchum**, **Robert Ryan** *and* **Joan Crawford**, *amongst others.*

legacy of self-pitying adolescence still haunts teenage bedrooms around the world. But cinema has been the richer for Brando's tortured life and the range of his work on screen rather than Dean's three movies and spectacular death.

TINSEL TALK

When Dustin Hoffman and Laurence Olivier worked together on *Marathon Man* (1976), they clashed over the Method. In one scene Hoffman's character was supposed to be knackered after being kept awake and tortured for days by Olivier's Nazi dentist. Hoffman prepared for the scene by staying awake for two days before shooting began, prompting Olivier to ask, 'Why doesn't the boy just act?'

1951 Australian sheep farmers introduce the myxomatosis virus to kill the rabbits eating their pastures.

1954 Teddy boys are big in the UK with narrow trousers, pointed shoes and long sideburns.

1956 The first televised advertisement in the UK is for Gibb's SR toothpaste.

1950s to the 1960s

Epics
Big Cast, Huge Budget

Ben-Hur (1969): even the lettering is epic.

Threatened with extinction at the hands of a 21-inch black-and-white TV set, Hollywood in its hour of need turned to God. In looking for the right vehicle to exploit their large range of widescreen formats, the studios reached for the Bible and epic tales of early Christianity to take them to the promised land of profitability. Biblically speaking, it was a numbers game, but what began as a revelation ended with an exodus.

After *The Robe* (1953), the first CinemaScope spectacle, it was left to Cecil B. DeMille to show the new breed how to do it. For his final film, he remade his own *The Ten Commandments* (1956), and in doing so happily obeyed Hollywood's first, returning a thumping $43 million on costs of $13.5 million. This success made the growth of the holy Roman epic an inevitability and *Ben-Hur* (1959) and *Spartacus* (1960) followed to great acclaim.

'I'm Spartacus!' Kirk Douglas produced and played the title role in *Spartacus*, alongside an all-star cast.

Co-Productions

By the 1960s, the epic was going down for the third time. But the studios still regarded them as prestige projects. As shooting costs were lower in Europe, Hollywood began co-producing pictures with continental backers, finding roles for stars from every participating country to boost the film's box-office chances. Mostly wartime adventures and Cold War thrillers, these Euro Puddings were a crude mix of travelogue and photo opportunity. Critics and audiences alike were less than impressed.

Naturally, the epic ethos could be applied to other topics. After the amiable *Around The World in 80 Days*, a travelogue pageant with an all-star cast, widescreen blockbusters sought out subject matter of heavyweight historical or literary significance, hence *War and Peace* (1956) and *El Cid* (1961).

1957 The Russians launch the first earth satellite, Sputnik I, and trigger the space race.

1962 The world hovers on the brink of atomic war when JFK has a stand-off with Fidel Castro in the Cuban Missile Crisis.

1967 In Britain, sexual intercourse between consenting men over the age of 21 is legalized.

TINSEL TALK

Mike Todd developed the Todd-AO single-camera process and produced *Around the World in 80 Days*, but it is as Elizabeth Taylor's third husband that he is remembered. Guests at their lavish 1957 wedding included Debbie Reynolds and her husband Eddie Fisher. Debbie couldn't have guessed that just over a year later Eddie would become the fourth Mr Taylor after Mike died when his private plane, the *Lucky Liz*, crashed in a storm.

Big money

Having lured viewers away from their armchairs, the studios were duty bound to put on a SHOW: widescreen, full-colour, stereo sound and an event movie. The blockbusters of the epic era ran and ran – *Around the World in 80 Days* for 210 minutes; *Exodus* for 3 hours, 33 minutes – but could generate massive profits. DeMille's *Ten Commandments* cost $13.5 million yet took nearly $43 million. But when they bombed, they left plenty of debris. Over 35 years on, the 243-minute *Cleopatra*, which took four years to make, still hasn't earned back its $40 million outlay, redefining previous studio notions of financial failure.

Elizabeth Taylor and Richard Burton met on the set of *Cleopatra*. He was to become both her fifth and her sixth husband.

Charlton Heston stars as Moses in *The Ten Commandments*.

To a director looking for cinematic immortality, the scale and scope offered by a lavish budget, almost unlimited running times and lush acres of unending cinema screen were an irresistible temptation. But the possibilities for failure were just as great. While David Lean demonstrated his mastery of the format with *Lawrence Of Arabia* (1962) and kept audiences, if not critics, happy with his follow-up *Dr Zhivago* (1965), others fared less well, and *El Cid* and *Mutiny On The Bounty* (1962) both lost money.

Cleopatra was the acme of the epic experience and a financial disaster that almost brought down 20th Century–Fox in its wake. The epic had finally reached its conclusion, not to be seen again in Hollywood for more than a decade, and then in a drastically revised form.

MOVIES – A CRASH COURSE **75**

1941 Jane Wyman and Regis Toomey set a new record when they kiss for three minutes and five seconds in the movie *You're in the Army Now*.

1944 Paris, the City of Romance, is liberated from Nazi Occupation.

1949 Giovanni Vigliotto begins his career as the world's greatest bigamist. Using a number of aliases he marries 104 times.

1940s and the 1950s
On the Town
Showstoppers

One man and one studio dominated the Hollywood musical in the 1940s and 1950s, an era which saw the genre reach both its artistic and commercial high-watermark. The studio was MGM and the man was Arthur FREED (1894–1973).

Gene Kelly and Frank Sinatra star in the spectacular musical *On the Town*.

Freed did not see himself as creative, although his background in vaudeville and track record as a successful lyricist at MGM would suggest otherwise. Nevertheless, his ability to spot and nurture talent was unrivalled. He championed the young Judy Garland and was a driving force behind *The Wizard Of Oz* (1939).

Judy Garland plays Dorothy in *The Wizard of Oz*, which had three different directors.

Freed also brought to MGM the man who was presently to become Garland's husband, *Vincente MINNELLI* (1903–1986). After a 2-year apprenticeship, Minnelli began a dazzlingly stylish directing career which in 1944 saw the release of *Meet Me In St Louis*. Minnelli went on to direct several non-musical films, but *An American In Paris* (1951), *The Band Wagon* (1953) and *Gigi* (1958) were prime examples of his artistic flair and the new trend for employing showstopping numbers to advance plot and character.

Hollywood during this period was countering the threat of television with ever more lavish productions – a process which stifled other genres but helped the musical – and MGM was brimming over with exceptional talent. *Gene KELLY* (1912–1996) graduated from being a performer into a highly successful

1951 The television series 'I Love Lucy' began, starring Lucille Ball and her husband Desi Arnaz.

1955 The cha-cha is imported from Cuba and its rapid triple step and changes of direction had people falling over themselves to try it.

1959 Flamboyant pianist Liberace wins damages from a London newspaper that claimed he was gay.

choreographer and director, working with Stanley Donen and creating three peerless musicals – *On The Town* (1949), *Singin' In The Rain* (1952) and *It's Always Fair Weather* (1955). *Singin' In The Rain* would probably rank as most people's favourite musical, while Gene Kelly's diluvial dancing remains one of cinema's iconic moments.

Where Freed had always looked to Broadway for his talent, other film companies now started to rely on lifting established shows intact from the Great White Way. Rodgers and Hammerstein's *Oklahoma!* (1955) paved the way for many more of their collaborations, a trend which reached its climax with their incredibly successful *The Sound Of Music* (1965). The spate of lavish musicals which sought to duplicate this success – *Dr Dolittle*, *Goodbye Mr Chips* – proved ruinously expensive, however, and virtually killed the genre stone dead.

Elvis with the cast off-set during filming of *Follow That Dream*.

ROLL THE CREDITS

Judy Garland *and* **Cyd Charisse** *(real names Frances Gumm and Tula Ellice Finklea) were regulars in MGM musicals, starring alongside* **Gene Kelly**, **Fred Astaire** *and* **Mickey Rooney**. *The studios often gave kids uppers and downers to make them fresh on set, and Judy became addicted. Her tortured life, five marriages, suicide attempts and alcoholism were legendary, in a career that ranged from Dorothy in* The Wizard of Oz *(1939) to Esther Blodgett in* **Cukor's** A Star is Born *(1954). When they needed a wholesome girl-next-door type, MGM called on* **June Allyson** *for musicals like* Best Foot Forward *and* Two Girls and a Sailor. *Universal gave her her best-known role opposite* **James Stewart** *in* The Glenn Miller Story.

Rock stars in the Movies

Elvis the Pelvis scowled like Brando, but that's where the similarities end. With the honorable exception of *Flaming Star* (1960), his films – with their flimsy plots and substandard show tunes – were strictly for fans. *A Hard Day's Night* (1964) was a different kettle of Fabs, a sort of pop goes the New Wave, while their psychedelic cartoon, *Yellow Submarine* (1968) remains the ultimate nostalgia trip. The Stones have put in some screen hours too, from Godard's intimate documentary *One Plus One* (1968) to the IMAX concert movie, *At the Max* (1992).

1952 The first car seat belts are manufactured in the US.

1954 Roger Bannister is the first man to run the mile in under 4 minutes.

1957 Gul Mohammed is born in India. At the age of 33, he measures less than 2 feet tall and weighs 2½ stone.

1950s and 1960s
Move Over, Darling
Romantic Comedy

The Cold War, impending nuclear holocaust and the England football team losing their unbeaten home record to Hungary – the 1950s weren't exactly the laughing decade, and humour at the cinema often seemed to be rationed like so many basic foodstuffs.

Doris is a career girl and Rock a womanizing songwriter in *Pillow Talk*.

The double act, the paradigm of screen comedy since the days of Laurel and Hardy, continued to hold sway. Foremost practitioners in the 1950s were Dean Martin and Jerry Lewis, who made 17 films together between 1949 and 1956 before ending their relationship in classic fashion – amidst bitter acrimony. Their routine was unwavering in films like *Sailor Beware* (1951) and *Scared Stiff* (1953), with Martin cast as the unflappable straight man trying to contend with Lewis' escalating wackiness. After their split, Martin found continued fame as a heavy-drinking fixture of light entertainment, while Lewis suffered the unenviable fate of being thought funny by the French, who dubbed him 'Le Roi Du Crazy'.

Romantic comedy, meanwhile, became the preserve of virgin queen, Doris Day, who with Rock Hudson and a succession of similar leading men delivered hugely formulaic but successful cosy courtship fare such as *Pillow Talk* (1959) and *Move Over Darling* (1963).

Another alliterative but, for many, more alluring blonde left a lasting mark on the comedies of the era. Marilyn Monroe's decade began with a memorable cameo in *All About Eve* (1950) and climaxed with the

Jerry Lewis and Dean Martin honed their act in nightclubs and theatres in the 1940s.

1960 Saxophonist Ornette Coleman introduces 'Free Jazz'.

1965 Mary Quant invents the mini skirt.

1968 The first British sextuplets are born in Birmingham.

sublime comedy of *Some Like It Hot* (1959). In between she laid the foundations for one of Hollywood's most enduring legends, with her irresistible mixture of voluptuous attraction combined with disarming naivety and underrated comic intuition. Monroe's films have been overshadowed by the troubles of her personal life, which culminated in her 'suicide' in 1962, but at her best she lived up to her maxim: 'I'm not interested in money. I just want to be wonderful.'

Monroe did her best work in the films of Austrian émigré Billy Wilder, deservedly recognized as one of the modern era's

Tony Curtis said kissing Marilyn in *Some Like It Hot* was like kissing Hitler.

> ### ROLL THE CREDITS
>
> **Rock Hudson, Doris Day** *and* **Marilyn Monroe** *were among the last stars to be moulded and manufactured by the studios. Aware that Hudson was gay, Universal arranged for him to marry his agent's secretary Phyllis Gates so the public wouldn't find out. Doris Day was typecast as the dizzy virgin and Monroe as the breathless sex kitten, and the studios tried to prevent them stepping outside these stereotypes. Since the collapse of the studio system, stars have been keen to demonstrate their versatility and have resisted the typecasting that was such a cornerstone of the Hollywood edifice.*

greats, whose versatility enabled him to create classics in many genres. After the influential noir *Double Indemnity* and the darkly satirical *Sunset Boulevard*, Wilder graduated to more conventional comedies, but always with a mordant edge. Compared to many of the sickly sweet Hollywood studio comedies of the 1950s, Wilder catered for a more mature taste and paved the way for the bolder efforts of a new era.

The Misfits

If any film can be seen as the last hurrah of the studio system, it's *The Misfits* (1961). Exhausted by strenuous stunts shot in the extreme heat of the Nevada desert, Clark Gable, the King of the Golden Age, died just days after shooting wrapped. Just over a year later, co star Marilyn Monroe (who had risen to the challenges in her then-husband Arthur Miller's difficult script) was also dead, but in much more mysterious circumstances. The hoodoo also hit Method acting pin-up Montgomery Clift, who made just one more film before dying of a heart attack in 1966 at the age of 46. Only the film's maverick director John Huston continued to prosper, completing his final feature, *The Dead* (1987), at the ripe old age of 80.

1951 British spies Burgess and Maclean skipped the country to avoid arrest and the mysteries began. Who was the third man? Was there a fourth?

1956 The Suez Crisis blew up when Egyptian president Gamal Abdel Nasser nationalized the Suez Canal, upsetting Britain, France and the US.

1959 The first hovercraft is tested at Cowes, and crosses the Channel in two hours.

1950s~mid 1960s
Double Bills and Drive-ins
Exploitation Movies

Beach Party paired Frankie Avalon and Annette Funicello.

'When 10,000 biceps meet 5,000 bikinis you know what's going to happen!' The poster tag line for Muscle Beach Party *(1964) is typical of the outrageous advertising which hallmarked the drive-in movies that emerged in the 1950s. Flushed with post-war success, American society had spawned a new breed of cinemagoers: young, with money in their pockets and almost all with access to a car. With the strictures against sex and violence loosening by the minute, the more entrepreneurial movie producers spied a killing to be made.*

Where the Boys Are (1960) explored the usual beach movie themes.

Most of the films that filled the drive-ins and small cinemas across America were exploitation pieces. An audience of thrill-hungry teens was served up a diet of sex, horror, juvenile delinquency and violence, accompanied by a maelstrom of over-the-top publicity that always promised more than it delivered. Shocking exposés of America's youth such as *Bad Girl* (1947), *Unwed Mother* (1958) and *Riot In Juvenile Prison* (1959) vied with cheap horror flicks, including *I Was A Teenage Werewolf* (1957) and freakish sex pieces such as *Glen Or Glenda?* (1953), a cross-dressing shockumentary directed by Ed Wood Jnr.

With quick money in the offing, it's hardly surprising that showmen dominated the exploitation/drive-in industry. Kroger

Babb, an ex-sports journalist, made his fortune touring dubious 'educational' films such as *She Shoulda Said No* and *Devil's Weed* (both *c.* 1950), and promoting them with sex-segregated screenings and educational pamphlets. But the most successful of the exploitation studios was

1963 Martin Luther King organizes a march on Washington and tells the marchers 'I Have a Dream'.

1965 Dr Zhivago enters the annals of movie history as one of the films most likely to make you cry.

1966 Walt Disney, the father of Donald Duck, Mickey Mouse and Goofy, dies in California.

American International Pictures. Set up by James H. Nicholson and Samuel Z. Arkoff in 1954 with just $3,000 capital. AIP specialized in double bills (often producing the posters before they did the movies). Most successful among their trash pic cycles were the beach movies. Starting with *Beach Party* (1963) and ending four films after with *How To Stuff a Wild Bikini*

ROLL THE CREDITS

An unholy partnership formed when low-budget producer **Roger Corman** *met archetypal villain* **Vincent Price** *and they began to explore their mutual admiration for the stories of* **Edgar Allan Poe**. *Films like* The House of Usher, The Pit and the Pendulum, Tales of Terror, The Masque of the Red Death *and* The Raven, *display an ironic sense of humour and a technical mastery that surpassed many other films in the genre. Great names such as* **Floyd Crosby** *and* **Nicolas Roeg** *worked on the cinematography.*

Ed Wood Jr.

Being declared the director of the worst film ever made was probably the best thing that ever happened to Ed Wood Jr. *Plan 9 From Outer Space* (1956) is the movie, and it's the combination of cardboard sets, risible dialogue and Bela Lugosi being replaced halfway through after he died during production, that make it a treasure trove for bad movie fans. Wood's other classic was *Glen Or Glenda?*, a mostly incomprehensible but for its time daring treatment of cross-dressing (a fetish of Wood's). He was the subject of an Oscar-winning biopic starring Johnny Depp (*Ed Wood*, 1994), but tragically did not live to enjoy the fame he had always sought.

Wood's *Plan 9* sank on release but was revived by Michael Medved in the 80s.

(1965), these movies delivered featherweight plots, bad music and acres of adolescent flesh – with not a mom or pop in sight.

There were certainly more serious movies made about the newly invented teenager and *The Wild One* (1954) and *Rebel Without A Cause* (1955) represented the major studios' response to the mania for youth-oriented flicks, but by the mid-1960s the world was changing rapidly. Drugs, rock n' roll, hippies and protest were the new youth watchwords, and the pantomime horror of teenage monsters and squeaky clean beach-partying kids looked increasingly like things from a different age.

Masque of the Red Death (1964) stars Vincent Price as a devil-worshipper.

1940 Duels are outlawed in Germany, long after they have disappeared in the rest of Europe and the US.

1942 Field Marshal Erwin Rommel is defeated by British forces at El Alamein.

1943 Welles and his new wife Rita Hayworth entertain troops at war.

1940s
Stiff Upper Lips and Coronets
British War Movies

The immediate threat of Nazi invasion threw British cinema – along with the rest of the country – into upheaval, as it strove to find ways to shore up the fragmenting spirits of a nation other than with the naive, lightweight comedies of George Formby, Will Hay and Arthur Askey. The relentlessly cheery trio did their bit, but mercifully Britain's homespun film fare did appear in other guises to help the war effort.

Olivier directs and plays the title role in a patriotic version of *Henry V* (1944).

The three branches of the services were each given stiff upper-lip salutes: *In Which We Serve* (navy), was followed by Carol Reed's much better *The Way Ahead* (army) and Anthony Asquith's *The Way To The Stars* (RAF). Meanwhile, Humphrey Jennings provided a stirring view of the home front in such films as *Fires Were Started*, which mixed narrative and a documentary flavour to excellent effect.

How we won the war

Not only did the Brits make umpteen patriotic movies during the course of the war but they kept on winning it for years after, right up until the 60's. Some films related true stories that couldn't be told at the time – *The Bridge on the River Kwai, The Colditz Story, The Dambusters, Battle of Britain* – while others, such as *The Dirty Dozen*, were more in keeping with the gung-ho comic-strip heroics that typified Hollywood's wartime flagwavers.

Wartime austerity (which at first saw cinemas close, and then the imposition of an entertainment tax) only heightened filmgoers' tastes for escapism. Gainsborough Studios' *The Wicked Lady* (all plunging necklines) and David Lean's *Brief Encounter* (all buttoned-up restraint) were both released on the same day in 1945; the former proved a huge hit, and the latter went on to achieve cult status.

Enid Stamp-Taylor and Margaret Lockwood in *The Wicked Lady* (1945).

1946 The Cannes Film Festival is founded, to promote tourism on the Côte d'Azur.

1947 Italo Calvino's first novel, *The Path to the Nest of Spiders*, is published and he is hailed as a Neo-Realist.

1948 The Selective Service System is introduced in the US, whereby you can get out of military service if you marry and have children young, or go to college.

ROLL THE CREDITS

Heir to a flour business, **J. Arthur Rank** *became interested in the film industry in the early 30s. He built Pinewood Studios, bought the Odeon and Gaumont cinemas, and formed a number of production companies that made* Henry V *and* Brief Encounter.

Frank Launder *and* **Sidney Gilliat** *were one of the most successful film-making teams of the 40's and 50's. In addition to scripting Hitchcock's* The Lady Vanishes *(1938), they were also the brains behind the five St Trinian's comedies.*

And the **Boulting Brothers John and Roy,** *were producer/directors of such British classics as* Brighton Rock *(1947),* Lucky Jim *(1957) and the* **Peter Sellers'** *vehicle* **I'm All Right, Jack** *(1959).*

Perhaps Britain's best wartime film, however, was to come from its most traditional source. Laurence Olivier's adaptation of *Henry V* (1944) was not just the ultimate morale-booster, it also defined Shakespeare on film for a generation, and prompted a revival in the fortunes of the literary adaptation. Two giants of English cinema were instrumental in this movement.

Screening the Bard

Shakespeare's not always been given the credit he deserves – a caption for *The Taming of the Shrew* (1929) read 'Additional dialogue by Sam Taylor'. Orson Welles mixed history and comedy plays for *Chimes at Midnight* (1966), while Kenneth Branagh got a Screenplay Oscar for not altering a word of *Hamlet* (1996). As Baz Luhrmann's street-smart *Romeo and Juliet* (1997) proves, where reinterpretation is concerned it's no holds Bard. *Macbeth* has been a Mafioso, *King Lear* a Japanese warlord and *Othello* a Wild West rancher.

Ann Valery, Alec Guinness and Dennis Price in *Kind Hearts and Coronets* (1949).

David Lean directed flawless versions of *Great Expectations* (1946) and *Oliver Twist* (1948), while Carol Reed cemented his reputation with two Graham Greene adaptations, *The Fallen Idol* (1948) and, unforgettably, *The Third Man* (1949).

British cinema continued to improve after the Second World War, particularly in the field of comedy, as the vibrant efforts of Michael Balcon's Ealing Studios and their star, Alec Guinness, demonstrated with the mordant black comedy, *Kind Hearts And Coronets* (1949). By the mid-1950s a new breed of film-maker was promising a similar revolution for the rest of British cinema.

1926 Prince Hirohito is crowned Emperor of Japan.

1950 The first Japanese tape recorder, produced by Tokyo Tsushin Kogyo (Sony), weighs nearly 40 pounds, uses tape made from rice paper, and sells for nearly $500.

1963 Weight Watchers is founded by a New York housewife. She has reduced her own weight from 213 to 142 pounds.

1920s to present

The Sun Rises

Japanese Cinema

Name a Japanese film made before 1950. Don't be too downhearted. Even experts would be hard-pushed to come up with half a dozen that they'd actually seen. When the West discovered Japanese cinema in the early 1950s, it had a lot of catching up to do. In addition to Expressionist silents such as Teinosuke Kinugasa's A Page of Madness *(1926), it had totally overlooked the likes of master film-makers Kenji* MIZOGUCHI *(1898–1956) and Yasujiro* OZU *(1903–1963). Critics couldn't tell a samurai from a* yakuza *and as for* jidai-geki *and* gendai-geki – *forget it.*

Kagemusha won the Palme d'Or at Cannes in 1980.

Anime films
Inspired by manga ('irresponsible pictures') comic books, anime films have been the sole bright spot amidst the gloom hanging over Japanese cinema. Long popular on TV before the international success of Katsuhiro Otomo's *Akira* (1987), anime films come in many guises. But the cult following is for violent futuristic tales in which teenagers thwart the schemes of dictatorial rulers.

*A*kira KUROSAWA (1910–) caused the kerfuffle. Telling the story of a murder from four different viewpoints, *Rashomon* (1950) deftly disproved the old myth that the camera never lies. A firm fan of John Ford, Kurosawa based *Seven Samurai* (1954) on the Hollywood western and had the favour returned with John Sturges' *The Magnificent Seven* (1960). Similarly, another samurai adventure, *Yojimbo* (1961), was reworked as the spaghetti western, *A Fistful of Dollars* (1964). Whether adapting Shakespeare (*Throne of Blood*, 1957 and *Ran*, 1985), surveying the contemporary scene (*Ikuru*, 1952) or recreating long-gone eras

(*Kagemusha*, 1980), Kurosawa has been most people's image of Japanese cinema for half a century.

But there are those who argue he's the least Japanese film-maker of the lot. Compare his dynamic style with that of Mizoguchi or Ozu. Influenced by the ancient art of scroll-painting, Mizoguchi's *The Story of the Late Chrysanthemums* (1939) and *The Life of Oharu* (1952) are both powerful studies of women's role in society and elegant examples of mise en scène. Ozu's *I Was Born But...* (1932) and

1968 A motorcycle gang in Tokyo raid the equivalent of £1 million from a security van and are never caught.

1976 Japanese authorities arrest former prime minister Kakuei Tanaka on charges that he accepted a $1.6 million bribe from Lockheed Aircraft Corp.

1983 David Bowie stars in the movie *Merry Christmas, Mr Lawrence*, about English soldiers held prisoner by the Japanese in Java.

Adapted from a popular comic strip, *Akira* is set in a violent Tokyo of the future.

ROLL THE CREDITS

One of many to have his early work censored by American forces in the late 1940s, **Kon Ichikawa** *eventually won many awards in the West. His post-war films focus on bleak themes like cannibalism and the horror of battle.* **Toshiro Mifune** *is the best-known Japanese actor in the West because of his long association with Kurosawa. However, Japanese audiences would more readily recognise* **Kyoshi Atsami**, *who played the wandering pedlar Tora-san in over 45 whimsical features.*

Tokyo Story (1953), on the other hand, are unique in their use of screen space, static, low-level cameras and 'pillow shots' – short poetic digressions that allow the viewer latitude to contemplate what they've just seen.

The problem of identifying the essential Japanese style arose again during the New Wave of the 1960s. Although they all agreed that modern society was the pits, each new director had their own approach. The most radical director was *Nagisa Oshima* (1932–), but not even provocative pictures like *Death by Hanging* (1968) and *In the Realm of the Senses* (1976) could tempt audiences away from *yakuza*, Godzilla, comic-book heroes and porn stars.

Since the mid-1970s, TV, Hollywood blockbusters and video have plunged Japanese cinema deep into crisis. Manga is the one bright spot on a horizon where the sun is rapidly setting.

A Page of Madness tells of an elderly man who works in the lunatic asylum where his wife is confined, using flashbacks to analyse the nature of insanity.

1928 André Breton issues the 'Manifesto of Surrealism', which calls for artists to create art of the subconscious.

1959 *Ben-Hur* is awarded eleven Oscars, the most ever won by a single film.

1964 The Surgeon General of the US Public Health Service issues a warning that most lung-cancer deaths are caused by cigarette smoking.

1928~1981
The Profound and the Profane
Bergman and Buñuel

The famous razor slicing an eyeball.

One was the son of a chaplain to the Swedish royal family, the other was raised as a Spanish landowner. One was a die-hard Surrealist, the other a lapsed Neo-Realist. One made serious films on such personal themes as faith, anguish and death, the other made satires on the sexual repression of the middle classes and the hypocrisy of the Catholic Church. One is synonymous with mischief, the other with gloom. Yet both were auteurs *who gave us a better understanding of ourselves and all our imperfections.*

L uis BUÑUEL (1900–1983) began making films in collaboration with the painter Salvador Dali in the late 1920s. *Un Chien Andalou* (1928) and *L'Age d'Or* (1930) were caustic Surrealist satires that grossly offended their audiences. Naturally, the pair considered them artistic triumphs. Yet Buñuel achieved precious little over the next two decades until his uncompromising portrait of slum life, *Los Olvidados* (1950). Then, suddenly, there was no end to his creativity as he produced 27 films in as many years. Lust simmered just below the surface in *El* (1952), *Belle de Jour* (1967) and *Tristana* (1970). Blasphemous irony was to the fore in *Nazarín* (1958) and *Viridiana* (1961), while middle-class conformity was held up to ridicule in *The Exterminating Angel* (1962) and *The Discreet Charm of the Bourgeoisie* (1972). Yet for all his sardonic

Bengt Ekerot as Death plays with Max von Sydow in *The Seventh Seal*.

Tax traumas
Persecuted by the taxman, Bergman stormed out of Sweden in 1976, claiming that he was being hounded like 'a vulgar importer of perishables'. Police arrested him during rehearsals for Strindberg's *Dance of Death* at Sweden's National Theatre after accusations that he owed back taxes. He remained in exile in Germany for 3½ years until an apology was forthcoming.

1970 The Beatles split up; fans blame Linda McCartney and Yoko Ono.

1974 Swedish super-group Abba win the Eurovision song contest with the irritating hit 'Waterloo'.

1978 *Interiors* is the first of Woody Allen's humourless tributes to Ingmar Bergman. It is followed by *September* (1987) and *Another Woman* (1988).

Catherine Deneuve plays a bored doctor's wife who works in a brothel just for kicks in *Belle de Jour*.

humour, Buñuel was in many ways an indulgent critic, recognizing that he shared many of the foibles he lampooned.

Breaking into films as a scriptwriter, *Ingmar BERGMAN* (1918–) forged his reputation with Neo-Realist films such as *Summer with Monika* (1952), which focused on loneliness, young love, the hellishness of life – or all three. With *The Seventh Seal* (1957) and *Wild Strawberries* (1958), symbolic films about humanity's place in God's grand plan, he became the darling of the art houses.

But no sooner had Bergman decided we had grounds for hope than he plunged us into the pessimism that hung heavily over the 'Chamber Play' trilogy of the early 1960s. Although he continued to work with the same stock company, a new stylistic boldness and a shift in emphasis became evident in his work from the moment he switched cinematographers (from Gunnar Fischer to Sven Nykvist) in 1963. *Persona* (1966), the 'Faro' trilogy and *Cries and Whispers* (1972) were more

concerned with questions of identity, alienation and communication – what one critic described as a 'smorgasbord of sex, sin and psychiatry'.

Although 'in retirement' since the acclaimed epic *Fanny and Alexander* (1982), Bergman has continued to write, completing yet another trilogy, this time based on his own family.

L'Age d'Or
Having sliced an eyeball and had ants pour from a hand wound in *Un Chien Andalou*, Buñuel had his work cut out to find similarly shocking material for *L'Age d'Or*. Some skeletal bishops, a cow on a bed and a woman performing fellatio on a statue's toe had the desired effect. At the première, members of a fascist group interrupted screening with chants of 'Death to the Jews!' and the screen was splattered with ink. There was also damage to an exhibition of paintings by Dali, Miro, Max Ernst and Man Ray in the theatre. The film was banned by the government.

ROLL THE CREDITS
Bergman *liked to work with familiar faces. So* **Max von Sydow, Liv Ullmann, Bibi Andersson** *and* **Gunnar Björnstrand** *became something of a personal stock company. The nomadic* **Buñuel**, *on the other hand, hired such fellow countrymen as* **Fernando Rey**, *Mexicans like* **Silvia Pinal** *and French stars of the calibre of* **Michel Piccoli, Jeanne Moreau** *and* **Catherine Deneuve.**

1924 Mahatma Gandhi goes on hunger strike to try to persuade Hindus and Muslims to stop fighting each other.

1957 Sitar player Ravi Shankar tours the world, popularizing Indian music, and inspires other musicians ranging from the Beatles to Yehudi Menuhin and André Previn.

1959 India gets her first television; villagers travel for hundreds of miles to visit six community TV centres at New Delhi where mounted police are required to keep the crowds away from the receivers.

1920s to the present
Bollywood and Beyond
Indian Cinema

India boasts the world's largest film industry. Only Hollywood and Germany could match its annual 50–100 movie turnover during the late silent era, but from the early 1960s, it's left all comers standing. Since 1980, India has averaged over 800 features per year, ¼ of the planet's movie output. Many of them come from the 'Bollywood' studios based in Bombay, but at least 26 regional language cinemas also flourish. Over 10 per cent of a population of 800 million go to the pictures each week, and nearly all of them are obsessed with 'masala' musicals, with their 'one star, six songs and three dances' formula.

Lights! Camera! Action!

Historicals, mythologicals, socials, melodramas, comedies and action films are the long-standing staples of Indian main-stream cinema. The vast majority of movies in these genres mix and match such elements as social or religious injustice, divided families, hidden identities, guilty secrets, frustrated romance and that invaluable standby, coincidence. But key to the success of most Indian movies are the ever-popular songs, which are invariably dubbed by 'playback singers', who often become as famous as their on-screen counterparts.

Kasauti (1989) is a classic Indian musical of the type exported worldwide.

Ray directs his leading man in *The Chess Players* (1977).

B ut – and here's a surprise – students of world cinema aren't the slightest bit interested in sentimental melodramas, mythologicals, historicals or stunt films. Instead they pore over pictures in which production numbers are supplanted by socio-political significance and escapist extravagance gives way to earnest realism.

Satyajit RAY (1921–1992) was responsible for bringing Indian cinema to an international audience. His *Apu Trilogy*

1975 Indira Gandhi is found guilty of electoral corruption. She responds by declaring a state of emergency and arresting her opponents.

1985 David Lean produces a film of E.M. Forster's *A Passage to India*, bringing international recognition to veteran actress Peggy Ashcroft.

1989 *Satanic Verses* by Bombay-born author Salman Rushdie is banned in India. In Iran, the Ayatollah Khomeini issues a fatwa.

ROLL THE CREDITS

Known as the 'Indian DeMille', **Raj Kapoor** *combined masala spectacle with social comment in films like* The Vagabond *(1951) and* Mr 420 *(1955). His regular co-star was* **Nargis**, *an actress who began her career as child star Baby Rani. She later became an MP and was one of the chief critics of* **Satyajit Ray's** *apolitical stance. Raj's brother,* **Shashi Kapoor**, *became known in the West for his collaborations with Merchant-Ivory, including* Bombay Talkie *(1970) and* Heat and Dust *(1982).*

The Apu trilogy include *Pather Panchali* (1955), *Aparajito* (1956) and *The World of Apu* (1959). *Apur Sansar* played the Bengali boy Apu.

(1955–1959), a 'rites of passage' story centred on a Bengali boy, Apu, owed much to Renoir and Neo-Realism. Soon his style and his themes diversified, focusing on cultural transition in *The Music Room* (1958), family life in *Kanchenjunga* (1962), the role of women in *Charulata* (1964)

and the corrupting influence of modern life in *Days and Nights in the Forest* (1969). Accused by some of glossing over India's social problems, Ray added a political (often satirical) edge to such later films as *Distant Thunder* (1973) and *Home and the World* (1982).

Ray split Indian film into two camps – Bollywood and Parallel Cinema. He remains the best-known subcontinental director, although disciples such as Mrinal Sen (*Mr Shome*, 1969) and Ritwik Ghatak (*Reason, Debate and a Tale*, 1974) became firm festival favourites.

Nothing could challenge the supremacy of the masala, however. The spread of TV has seen admissions drop in the 1990s, but Bollywood has found a new source of income from exporting its movies to exiled Indian communities around the world. With all this commercial clout, it remains a mystery why, in an artform as cross-referential as cinema, the masala has been so neglected by so many for so long.

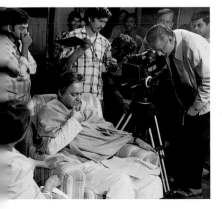

Ray films *An Enemy of the People* (1981), adapted from the Ibsen original.

1950s In the early years of the decade, missionaries report that open cannibalism has more or less ceased in Papua New Guinea.

1956 Jackson Pollock dies in a car accident in Long Island. His depressive painting of the last few years tends to feature paint dripped or hurled onto the canvas.

1958 Eight Manchester United football players are killed in an air crash, along with five substitutes and eight journalists.

1950s~1960s
Gothic
Hammer House of Horror

In *Witchfinder General*, set in 1645, a profit-seeking lawyer travels the country conducting witch hunts.

The British have always had a slightly queasy relationship with horror on the big screen. During the days of the great Universal horror movies (such as Dracula *and* Frankenstein*) in the 1930s, the British censor banned a number of the films. But in the 1950s and 1960s a small studio located at Bray, Berkshire, was to dominate the international horror market.*

Two classics released by Hammer Films in 1958 and 1973.

Hammer Films had been around for more than two decades before it scored its first horror hit, *The Curse of Frankenstein* (1957). Terence Fisher directed Christopher Lee and Peter Cushing in the movie, which provoked a slew of outraged articles in the press. Its major innovation was to return the sensuality to Mary Shelley's classic tale and to introduce full-colour blood to the screen for the first time (the unnaturally bright red concoction used was called 'Kensington gore', after its place of manufacture). A year later, Fisher would tackle *Dracula*, and bring to it the same sexual undercurrents and, at the time, shockingly grisly effects; while Christopher Lee would jettison Bela Lugosi's theatrical interpretation in favour of a sensual and seductive version of the role.

The Curse of the Werewolf (1960) and *The Phantom of the Opera* (1962) were among the movies that the studio subsequently produced until it made its final horror film, *To The Devil A Daughter*, in 1971 and moved into television with the anthology shows *Hammer House Of Horror* (1980).

In the wake of American slashers such as *The Texas Chainsaw Massacre* (1974) and *Friday The 13th* (1980), the films may look tame, even campy, but for the time they were ground-breaking in the talent that they employed in the horror genre. Many of the trademarks of Hammer movies would turn up in Italian 'giallo' films (literally 'yellow', after the colour of

1964 *Mary Poppins* is the biggest hit of the year and the most popular live action film Disney has made.

1969 Charles Manson is convicted of the gruesome murders of Sharon Tate and six of her friends near Bel Air.

1977 Christopher Lee's autobiography, *Tall, Dark and Gruesome*, is published.

the spines of the pulp thriller novels on which some of them were based). Dario Argento and Mario Bava, the key directors in the cult genre, used the same melodramatic plots and gut-churning gore in films like *Suspiria* (1977) and *Black Sunday* (1960) and would even borrow Hammer rep members Boris Karloff for *Black Sabbath* (1963) and Lee for *Night Is The Phantom* (1963). In the wake of Hammer's runaway success, a couple of horror companies attempted to steal some of its thunder. Amicus made its name with anthology movies such as *Dr Terror's House Of Horrors* (1964), in which several

Screen Frankensteins

Augustus Phillips was the first screen Frankenstein in 1910 with Charles Ogle as the monster; Boris Karloff was made 18 inches taller and 65 pounds heavier to play the monster in the 1931 *Frankenstein*, directed by James Whale; while Bela Lugosi finally played him in *Frankenstein Meets the Wolf Man* (1943). Peter Cushing was Hammer's mix-and-match madman, while Kenneth Branagh was responsible for Robert De Niro's eloquent creature in *Mary Shelley's Frankenstein* (1994). And Frank. N. Furter timewarps his way through the *Rocky Horror Picture Show* (1975).

Doug Bradley stars as Pinhead in Clive Barker's *Hellraiser* (1987).

ROLL THE CREDITS

With his bulging eyes and balding pate, **Donald Pleasance** *was one of the most disconcerting villains Britain ever produced. An actor with a dangerous edge, he is particularly remembered for* **Roman Polanski's** Cul-de-Sac *(1966) and* **John Carpenter's** Halloween *(1978). Europe had its fair share of horror meisters, ranging from the classy (***Georges Franju's** Eyes Without a Face, *1959) to the trashy (just about anything directed by* **Jésus Franco, Jean Rollin** *or* **José Larraz**). *Japanese horror was dominated by* **Inishiro Honda's** *'creature features', starring that prehistoric hero par excellence,* Godzilla.

stories comprise the film, while Tigon produced the genuinely shocking *Witchfinder General* (1968), directed by the tragically short-lived Michael Reeves and starring Vincent Price.

Recently, Britain appears to have left horror to other countries, but Bernard Rose, who made the innovative child's nightmare movie *Paperhouse* (1989) and *Candyman* (1992), adapted from a novel by British horror writer Clive Barker, is one hope for the future, while Barker himself turned to directing with *Hellraiser* (1987).

1957 The documentary *City of Gold*, about the Klondike gold rush, uses a camera ranging across 19th-century landscape photos in an innovative new technique.

1962 De Gaulle negotiates a settlement freeing Algeria from French rule.

1963 Formation of the Rolling Stones, whose lead singer Mick Jagger is known for his rubber lips and swivelling hips.

1950s and 1960s
Nouvelle Vague
French Post-war Cinema

'Cinéma du papa' – that was what they called the films made in post-war France. Elegant, literate, impeccably played and quite entertaining... in a Hollywood sort of way. Predictably, the critics of the French journal Cahiers du cinéma *loathed them – these glossy talkfests were the work of artisans, not artists! Fired up by the* auteur *theories of Alexandre Astruc and André Bazin, young turks like François* TRUFFAUT *(1932–1984) and Jean-Luc* GODARD *(1930–) denounced anyone outside their hall of fame. If you lacked the individuality of Welles, Rossellini, Hawks or Nicholas Ray, then your chances of a rave review in* Cahiers *were non-existent.*

Working in Tinseltown

European artists are lured to Hollywood by the promise of filthy lucre, and international recognition, but many find their artistic integrity compromised. Not Louis Malle. He was one of the few post-war directors to achieve real success in both Europe and America, and he didn't change his artistry or subject matter one iota, exploring extremes of human behaviour such as child prostitution, incest, and life in Occupied France.

Some home-based directors were admitted to the outer portals. Jean Cocteau (*Orphée*, 1950) was a poetic fantasist, Max Ophüls (*Lola Montès*, 1955) waltzed with the camera. Robert Bresson stripped away such cinematic 'essentials' as drama and performance in sparse features like *The Diary of a Country Priest* (1950), while Jacques Tati revived the lost art of slapstick and shattered the rules of screen storytelling in *Monsieur Hulot's Holiday* (1953) a tale of mishaps au bord de la mer.

Despite these efforts, too few French film-makers were willing to break from the detested 'Tradition of Quality', and so the *Cahiers* crowd went into production themselves. If you're watching a black-and-white French film in which the picture looks like it's got the DTs, the action keeps hiccuping and everyone talks slowly and seriously without actually saying very

1964 Britain and France agree to build a tunnel under the English Channel.

1968 Students riot in Paris and occupy public buildings, over a complex series of grievances.

1971 France's chicest woman Coco Chanel dies. She was famous for popularizing the little black dress, worn with Chanel No. 5 perfume.

Lights! Camera! Action!

On the surface the stylistic hijinks of the New Wave seem merely mischievous. But jerky handheld camera shots, sudden shifts in logic ('jump cuts') and the use of direct sound, natural light and location settings came a lot closer to capturing the rhythms of modern life than silky Hollywood escapism. Such tactics also ensured that you could never forget you were watching a work of art and not a slice of life. What's more, they allowed the director to follow Astruc and Bazin's advice and use the camera in as personal a way as a writer would use a pen.

Jules et Jim et Catherine (Oskar Werner, Henri Serre and Jeanne Moreau) in Truffaut's lyrical tribute to a tragi-comic menage à trois (1961).

ROLL THE CREDITS

They say that those that can do and those that can't become critics. But in the case of the Cahiers *critics, many went on to make their mark as artists with such great films as* **Claude Chabrol's** Les Cousins, **Jacques Rivette's** Paris Belongs to Us *and* **Eric Rohmer's** My Night with Maud.

Agnes Varda, *whose 1954 short* La Pointe courte *is widely considered the first New Wave film, worked in a fractured abstract style. However her husband,* **Jacques Demy**, *proved the heir to the Hollywood musical, with such chic entertainments as* The Umbrellas of Cherbourg.

much, then it's a safe bet it was made by a New Wave *auteur*.

Truffaut's early films, such as *The Four Hundred Blows* (1959) and *Jules et Jim* (1961) were packed with in-jokes and homages to heroes like Vigo, Hitchcock and Renoir. But, with the exception of *Day for Night* (1973), his work increasingly came to resemble the 'Quality' pictures he'd rubbished.

The same could not be said of Godard. From his B-Movie-inspired debut, *Breathless* (1959), it was clear a risk-taker was at work. By *Pierrot le fou* (1965) and

Weekend (1967), he was forever disrupting the action with printed slogans and speeches direct to camera. Over the next 30 years, flirtations with Maoism, Black Pantherism and video followed as Godard delighted in his reputation as modern cinema's *enfant terrible*.

But the *Cahiers* cronies were not the lone Wavers. Some, like Alain Resnais in the baffling *Last Year in Marienbad* (1961) played with time, space and stucture to find the film equivalent of modernist literature. The Nouvelle Vague ran out of steam by about 1963, by which time its knock-on effects were beginning to be felt around the world.

1946 Fox sign up a 20-year-old model called Norma Jean Baker at a salary of $75 a week. She later changes her name to Marilyn Monroe.

1961 Luciano Pavarotti makes his debut as Rodòlfo in Puccini's *La Bohême* at the Teatro Municipale in Reggio Emilia.

1965 Julie Andrews softens the iron-willed Baron von Trapp in the Austrian Hills and *The Sound of Music* goes on to win five Oscars.

1945~1970s
The Italian Job
Seduction and Blasphemy

Pasolini's *Decameron* (1971) was based on the tales by Boccaccio.

Reading most film histories, you'd think Hollywood mass-produced entertainment while the rest of the world handcrafted art. Not so. Nearly every film industry catered for its home market, mostly sponsoring vehicles for popular comics, and Italy's was no exception: its clown prince was one Antonio di Bisanzio, known to millions as Totò. But Italian cinema was unusual in that many of its main-stream movies also found an international audience.

Monica Vitti was the perfect Antonioni heroine in *L'Avventura*.

As production costs spiralled in the early 1950s, several Hollywood pictures were shot as 'runaways' at Rome's Cinecittà studios. Consequently, producers became familiar with such staples as the 'peplum' movies – adventures set in the ancient world starring such inanimate beefcakes as ex-Mr Universe Steve Reeves. By the 1960s, however, these 'sword and sandal' epics had become increasingly camp, and their box-office thunder was stolen by the spaghetti westerns of Sergio Leone, and the 'giallo' and horror flicks of Mario Bava and Dario Argento.

Yet it was Italian art cinema that produced the works of true genius. Pre-eminent in this second film renaissance

were *Michelangelo* ANTONIONI (1912–) and *Federico* FELLINI (1920–1993). The two shared the acclaim, but beyond their Neo-Realist heritage, little else.

Antonioni was the first to hit his stride, with his dispassionate studies of broken-hearted women alone in unfriendly cities (*Story of a Love Affair*, 1950 and *The Girlfriends*, 1955). Fellini, meanwhile, veered between the autobiographical (*I Vitelloni*, 1953) and the sentimental (*Nights of Cabiria*, 1957).

However, in 1960, both produced masterpieces. In *L'Avventura*, Antonioni all but abandoned narrative in a bold bid to express his characters' emotions almost exclusively through their environment.

1970 Germaine Greer's book *The Female Eunuch* abhors feminine archetypes and advocates sexual freedom

1975 Gunmen hold seven Italians hostage in a London restaurant, in what is known as the Spaghetti House Siege.

1978 Red Brigade terrorists murder Italian politician Aldo Moro. His bullet-ridden body is found in a car in the centre of Rome.

Fellini also experimented with a new style in his episodic satire, *La Dolce Vita*.

Over the next decade, Antonioni's work became increasingly controlled and cool as Fellini's became more personal and prone to excess. The 'Alienation' trilogy of *La Notte* (1960), *L'Eclisse* (1962) and *The Red Desert* (1964) revealed a conscious shift towards the abstract, while *8½* (1963), *Fellini-Satyricon* (1969) and *Amarcord* (1973) seemed to vindicate Orson Welles' opinion that Fellini was 'a superlative artist with little to say'.

Anita Ekberg and Mastroianni in *La Dolce Vita* (1960).

Decadence

Fellini and Pasolini chose stories from the past to mirror the depravity in contemporary life: *Casanova*, *The Decameron*, *Canterbury Tales* and *Satyricon*. They claimed to be reflecting life in their movies but the authorities accused them of sexual perversion and bringing the church into disrepute. Pasolini's life ended in similarly controversial circumstances. He was found on wasteland outside Ostia in 1975, having been beaten to death by a 17-year-old male prostitute.

ROLL THE CREDITS

Owner of the world's twinkliest eyes, equally at home as charming leading man or world-weary anti-hero, **Marcello Mastroianni** *was Italy's most internationally famous actor. Although director and ex-matinee idol* **Vittoria de Sica** *paired him with the voluptuous* **Sophia Loren** *in a string of romantic comedies, he was best known as the Muse of* **Federico Fellini.** **Monica Vitti** *fulfilled a similar role for* **Antonioni**, *although many critics have attacked him for using her as a cinematic chess piece.*

Sophia Loren starred opposite Cary Grant, Charlton Heston, Frank Sinatra and Peter Sellers, as well as Marcello Mastroianni.

There was also much to admire in the operatic grandeur of Luchino Visconti, the provocative poetry of Pier Paolo Pasolini and Bernardo Bertolucci's shifts from the political and personal to the spectacular: but the Italian film industry, like its French counterpart, is sadly no longer the centre of cinematic invention it once was.

It's nigh on forty years since Italy and France were among cinema's movers and shakers. Outstanding talents are still at large, notably Bernard Tavernier, Bertrand Blier and Luc Besson, Francesco Rosi, Ettore Scola and the Taviani brothers. But box-office hits like *Cinema Paradiso* are pretty rare. Yet that arch jackdaw Hollywood continues to rework Euro hits such as *True Lies* and *Scent of a Woman*.

1958 There are race riots in London's Notting Hill.

1960 John Bratby, English painter of the Kitchen Sink School, has a nervous breakdown, and changes to a lighter palette.

1960 The soap opera Coronation Street begins on British television.

1959~68

Kitchen Sink and Beyond
The Angry Young Men

Ken Loach's *Kes* features a boy and his bird.

Should one's recreational interests include getting drunk, playing rugby league, putting the girlfriend in the family way or killing a kestrel, 1960s British cinema offered vistas of unparalleled opportunity. Although Sir David continued to plough his epic furrow, the British New Wave blew away such stuffy Lean concerns as stoicism, militarism and the Empire in an orgy of political and sexual liberation and frightening regional accents. And then lost everything in a tidal wave of American money and rampant self-indulgence.

The success of John Osborne's furious diatribe *Look Back in Anger* (1959) at the Royal Court Theatre and Czech-born director Karel Reisz' film *Saturday Night and Sunday Morning* (1962), brimming over with anti-Establishment working-class Northern disaffection, sparked a brief but vibrant flowering of British talent, both in front of and behind the camera. Tony Richardson, John Schlesinger and Lindsay Anderson helmed the films which made stars of Albert Finney, Alan Bates, Tom Courtenay and Richard Harris. This being the 1960s, the revolution offered few vacancies for women.

Anarchy on the playing fields of Eton in *If...* (1967), class war in action.

But when Richardson and Osborne's Woodfall Films sought financial backing from United Artists to make *Tom Jones*, the British film industry was changed irrevocably. Disastrously, it proved a huge success, its bawdy concerns chiming with Philip Larkin's observation that 'sexual

1960 James Spader, Timothy Hutton, Sean Penn and Kenneth Branagh are born: angry young men for the next generation?

1962 Laurence Olivier is made director of the National Theatre, based at London's Old Vic.

1967 *The Graduate* pairs Anne Bancroft as Mrs Robinson and Dustin Hoffmann as the graduate in a film that excites college boys everywhere.

Working-class concerns

Britain's heritage, class system and housing estates have continued to serve its cinema well since the 1960s. The kitchen sink tradition was taken up by Ken Loach in *Kes* (1969) and later with *Riff-Raff* (1991). Mike Leigh is renowned for his detailed observations of working-class life in award-winning films like *Naked* (1993) and *Secrets and Lies* (1996). And the tradition has been updated with such films as *Trainspotting* (1995) and *The Full Monty* (1997) to reflect a society in transition.

intercourse began in 1963'. This alerted Hollywood to the money-making possibilities of Britain and, in particular, Swinging London. By 1968, 90 per cent of British first features were made with American money and as the dollars rolled in, reason made a swift exit.

Although the New Wave flag continued to flutter in the late 1960s with Lindsay Anderson's *If...* and Ken Loach's *Kes*, more typical products of the period were ghastly Michael Winner offerings such as *I'll Never Forget What's-'is'-Name* or the

Richard Burton, Tony Richardson and Gary Raymond in *Look Back in Anger*.

self-indulgent *Can Hieronymous Merkin Ever Forget Mercy Humppe And Find True Happiness*? By 1969 all the American studios were losing money. They made their excuses, and left Britain with the hangover of the three-day-week and the ever-diminishing returns on the Carry On series.

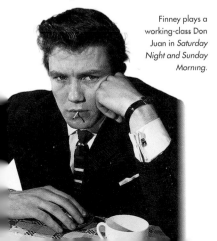

Finney plays a working-class Don Juan in *Saturday Night and Sunday Morning*.

ROLL THE CREDITS

The roots of social realism lay in the Free Cinema of the previous decade. Decisively non-commercial, films like **Karel Reisz's** We Are the Lambeth Boys *(1959) aimed to focus on the poetry of everyday life. Considering the Angry Young Man phase began on the stage, it's fitting that so many movie-makers furthered their careers in the theatre.* **John Schlesinger** *was an associate director at London's National Theatre from 1973;* **Tony Richardson** *was a central figure at the Royal Court and* **Lindsay Anderson** *was a key figure of British theatre in the 1970s to 1980s, premièring new plays at the Royal Court, Theatre Royal Stratford East and the Riverside.*

1969 It is found that the average frankfurter sold in the US has 33 percent fat and some are more than half fat.

1976 Ulrike Meinhof of the Baader-Meinhof gang hangs herself in jail. Her funeral attracts over 4,000 mourners, many with their faces painted white or wearing masks.

1980 John Lennon is shot dead by a deranged fan outside the Dakota building in New York.

1945 to the present
New German Cinema
Fassbinder, Herzog and Wenders

German cinema – as with all else – was in tatters in 1945. A few 'rubble' films about life in the bombed-out cities and the new East-West divide hardly amounted to a Neo-Realist revival. By the early 1960s, tired of cosy 'Heimat' movies and Hollywood imports, a band of budding film-makers hijacked the annual Oberhausen Film Festival to issue a manifesto calling for a 'Young German Cinema'. After years of lobbying, government grants were finally obtained and Germany's much delayed New Wave finally got under way.

Yet 'das neue Kino' found few friends at home. German audiences had only just got used to Hollywood's New-Wave-inspired rethink, and couldn't be bothered to wrestle with yet more innovations. Besides which, many of the films were openly critical of a society with which they were pretty comfortable. So the only plaudits came from critics and overseas cinéastes – although even they struggled to appreciate the far-from-conventional work of Hans Jurgen Syberberg and Jean-Marie Straub.

Much more in their line were the films of the prolific *Rainer Werner FASSBINDER* (1946–1982). Initially a disciple of Godard, he came to sugar his socialism with a surface gloss borrowed from the Ross Hunter produced melodramas of Douglas Sirk. Rattling cages as he went, he tackled such

> ### Mammoth movies
> Translating as the 'homeland film', the heimatfilm was one of the few thriving genres in post-war Germany. Extolling the virtues of rural life and invariably depicting love triumphing in the face of adversity, one of the best known was *Die Trapp-Familie* (1956), which told much the same story as *The Sound of Music* but without Julie Andrews. Much satirized in the 1960s, the genre was revitalised by Edgar Reitz's mammoth *Heimat* (1984). Yet its 924-minute running time was pipped by Fassbinder's 16¼ hour, 13-episode TV-movie *Berlin-Alexanderplatz* (1980).

Hanna Schugulla in *The Marriage of Maria Braun* (1978), directed by Fassbinder.

1985 Large quantities of Austrian wine are found to contain anti-freeze to make it sweeter.

1989 The Berlin Wall is knocked down. People sell lumps of rock as souvenirs.

1995 Bulgarian artist Christo wraps the Reichstag in 1 million square feet of silver fabric secured by 49,000 feet of blue rope.

no-go topics as racial and sexual prejudice, bourgeois decadence and political inertia in films that included *The Bitter Tears of Petra von Kant* (1972) and *Fear Eats the Soul* (1974). Yet his most provocative work dared to delve into Germany's Fascist past, notably in *Chinese Roulette* (1976) and *The Marriage of Maria Braun* (1978).

The American influence is also evident in the road movies of Wim Wenders, among them *Alice in the Cities* (1973) and *Paris Texas* (1984). Even though he dedicated *Wings of Desire* (1987) to Truffaut, Ozu and Tarkovsky, its chief influence is clearly Frank Capra's *It's a Wonderful Life*.

The maverick of the bunch was *Werner HERZOG* (1942–). Hailed as a 'romantic visionary', he produced mesmerizing

Bruno Ganz and Peter Falk in Wenders' *Wings of Desire* (1987), the director's homage to Truffaut.

studies of eccentrics driven to destruction by their overpowering obsessions. Also a challenging documentarist, Herzog was the master of the symbolic landscape – a barren wilderness in *Heart of Glass* (1976), a strange town in *Nosferatu the Vampyre* (1979) and a wild jungle in *Fitzcarraldo* (1982).

Sadly, no one of equal calibre emerged to build on the achievements of the 'das neue Kino'. Consequently, like so many others worldwide, German cinema currently languishes in the doldrums created by Hollywood's domination and its own indolence.

ROLL THE CREDITS

Alexander Kluge *was the driving force behind the new wave, although his own films, like* Yesterday Girl *(1966), were often overlooked. The first German director to make an international impact was* **Volker Schlöndorff**, *who later co-directed* The Lost Honour of Katharina Blum *(1975) with his wife* **Margarethe von Trotta**. *She emerged as a fine film-maker in her own right with* The Second Awakening of Christa Klages *(1978), while Schlöndorff won an Oscar for his adaptation of* The Tin Drum *(1979).*

Herzog's favourite actor, Klaus Kinski, plays the title role in *Nosferatu the Vampyre*.

99

1956 The Soviet Union suppresses the Hungarian Revolution.

1958 Chuck Berry releases Johnny B. Goode. Rock'n'roll dominates youth culture to parents' incomprehension.

1963 The nuclear-powered submarine *USS Thresher* sinks off Cape Cod killing all 129 men on board.

1950s to the 1980s

Political Protest
Cinema Behind the Iron Curtain

Tarkovsky was widely praised for *Andrei Rublev, Stalker, Polaris* and *The Mirror*.

Having suppressed the spirit of Soviet invention, Stalin set about subjecting the Communist bloc to his socialist-realist whims in the early 1950s. But the film-makers of Eastern Europe refused to knuckle under, and no sooner had one subversive surge been stifled than another would rise up in its place.

Cinematic creativity invariably went hand-in-hand with political protest. The 'New Course' films of Károly Makk and Zoltán Fábri heralded the Hungarian uprising of 1956. The de-Stalinization of Poland prompted the emergence of the 'Polish Film School', whose leading light, *Andrzej WAJDA* (1926–), forged an international reputation with the war trilogy that culminated in *Ashes and Diamonds* (1958).

Inevitably, the periodic clampdowns still resulted in casualties. The Georgian director *Sergei PARADJANOV* (1920–1990) so offended the authorities with the likes of *Shadows of Our Forgotten Ancestors* (1964) that he was

The Firemen's Ball is a sharp satire of Czech society that attracted wide acclaim.

forced to endure long periods of inactivity and even a spell in jail. Yet, in Hungary, Miklós Jancsó, who proved every bit as formalist in films like *The Red and the White* (1967), was hailed as a 'film poet' and allowed to prosper. Elsewhere, the Poles Jerzy Skolimowsky and Roman Polanski, and the Russians Andrei Konchalovsky and, eventually, Andrei Tarkovsky, were given permission to further their careers in the West. However, exile from home and family would, for Tarkovsky at least, prove a fatal sacrifice.

Nevertheless, you couldn't keep a good Slav down, as witnessed by the Czech New Wave that ushered in the Prague Spring of 1967–1969. Milos Forman (since safely ensconced in Hollywood) drew most attention for satires such as *The Firemen's Ball* (1967) that bore the

1974 Aleksandr Solzhenitsyn writes *The Gulag Archipelago*; he is immediately arrested by the KGB and expelled from the Soviet Union.

1980 Warren Beatty films the story of American Communist John Reed in *Reds*. It is his first attempt as a director.

1988 Soviet athletes win 132 medals at the Olympic games in Seoul. Canadian runner Ben Johnson is stripped of his medal and sent home in disgrace after failing a drugs test.

Puppets and folk tales

They're pretty big on animation in Eastern Europe. Inspired by the Russian genius Wladeslaw Starewicz, the puppet film has particularly flourished. The Czech Jiri Trnka combined parable, pantomime and parody to comment on the contemporary world in such folk tales as *The Emperor's Nightingale*. His compatriot Jan Svankmajer is markedly more savage in his satire, shedding a surreal light on such familiar tales as *Alice in Wonderland* and *Faust*. The Poles Walerian Borowczyk and Jan Lenica and the Yugoslav Vatroslav Mimica were among the many who started out making cartoons before turning to live-action features.

influence of just about every film movement since the Second World War. But normal service was soon resumed and several pictures were branded 'banned forever'. High-pointed by Dusan Makaveyev's *W.R. – Mysteries of the Organism* (1971), Yugoslavian Novi Film was similarly consigned to the historical dustbin by a spate of state-approved 'black' films.

Man of Iron tells of the life of a bricklayer hero of the 1950s who stepped out of line.

ROLL THE CREDITS

Many of the key figures in the Czech Film Miracle trained at the FAMU film school. **Vera Chytilová** *so annoyed the authorities with her surrealist comedy* Daisies *that she struggled to fund future projects.* **Jan Nemec's** *Kafkaesque* The Party and the Guests *was similarly frowned upon. Less controversial, although equally inventive, were films set during the war, like* **Jiri Menzel's** Closely Watched Trains *and* The Shop on the High Street, *directed by the non-FAMU duo,* **Jan Kadar** *and* **Elmar Klos**.

Cinema was finally to strike a decisive blow against Kremlin control during the Solidarity uprising of 1980–1981. Again Andrzej Wajda was to the fore with *Man of Iron* (1981), openly encouraging the cult of trade-union leader Lech Walesa; Agnieszka Holland (*Provincial Actors*, 1980), Krzysztof Zanussi (*The Constant Factor*, 1980) and Krzysztof Kieslowski (*Blind Chance*, 1981) also played key roles in this 'cinema of moral anxiety' that helped persuade a nation that toeing the Party line was no kind of future.

There were further signs of revival as the Iron Curtain rusted, notably the Serbian-based 'Prague Group' and the new Russian realism of the glasnost era. But the post-Communist withdrawal of state funding plunged Eastern Europe's unfettered film industries into deep crisis, from which there appears no easy way out.

1964 In Peru, 300 are killed in a stampede after a football match. Fans were unhappy about a disallowed goal.

1974 Henry Kissinger brokers an agreement whereby Israel withdraws from the west bank of the Suez Canal, Egypt reoccupies the east bank, and a UN buffer zone is created between the two.

1984 Lord of the Jungle Johnny Weissmuller dies. He played Tarzan between 1932 and 1948, and was also famous for winning 5 Olympic swimming medals and setting 67 world records.

1960s to the present

Global Cinema
Africa, Asia and South America

Unless you've been skipping pages, you will already have come across much to prove that there is life beyond planet Hollywood. Once solely the preserve of highbrow festivals and media studies courses, movies from the world's lower profile film industries now crop up regularly on video and TV. Some have come to command loyal international followings, while others struggle to find space even on the domestic screen.

Ousmane Sembene's *Xala* (1974) raised the international profile of African cinema.

Film festivals

There are now over 90 major film festivals worldwide, as well as hundreds more minor ones. In addition to the big three – Cannes, Berlin and Venice – there are festivals for documentaries, animation, shorts, kidpix, feminist films and a range of contemporary issues. Some award prizes, most include tribute seasons to big-name directors. Occasionally Hollywood hijacks the main Euro bashes to boost forthcoming blockbusters. But the ones that don't make the tabloids do a vital job in putting the films of lesser-known directors in the spotlight. Who needs an Oscar when you can win the Golden Spike of Valladolid?

Not all films travel well. With the exception the Iranian director, Abbas Kiarostami, and Egyptian Youssef Chahine, Islamic cinema has attracted little attention in the West. Cultural insularity and the mechanisms motivating the distribution networks have meant that much cinema from the developing world passes us by.

In truth, we're only familiar with the odd outstanding film-maker rather than entire national traditions. We may have heard of Hou Hsiao-Hsien, but know next to nothing about Taiwanese cinema. Similarly with Emilio Fernandez from Mexico, Lino Brocka (Philippines) and Raúl Ruiz (Chile).

In the 1960s, a number of Latin Americans harnessed the techniques of the Nouvelle Vague to their campaigns for political liberation. In their 'third cinema' manifesto, the Argentines Fernando E. Solanas and Octavio Getino advocated 'guerrilla' film-making, a cry taken up by Brazilian directors Glauber Rocha and Ruy Guerra during the 'cinema nôvo' era. Film still had a pro-government purpose, however, as witnessed in Cuba (although there was often a hint of sly satire in the work of Tomas Gutierrez Alea).

1986 Corrupt dictator Ferdinand Marcos is forced out of the Philippines. World media try to count his wife Imelda's shoe collection.

1990 71-year-old Nelson Mandela is released from jail in South Africa after 27 years in captivity.

1996 The population of China is estimated to be 1.22 billion, which is more than that of the whole world 150 years ago.

ROLL THE CREDITS

Gong Li *debuted in* Red Sorghum *(1987), one of six films she made with one-time partner Zhang Yimou.* **Maggie Cheung** *flits between art-house and films with Jackie Chan, while* **Michelle Yeoh**'s *martial artistry led to a role in the Bond movie* Tomorrow Never Dies. *Combining chop socky and steamy sex,* **Amy Yip** *is the star of soft-core porn movies with a kick.*

A decade on, and Black African film came of age. The key figure here is the Senegalese Ousmane Sembene, but other former French colonies have also prospered, including Mali (Souleymane Cissé), Burkina Faso (Idrissa Ouedraogo) and Mauritania (Med Hondo).

The 1980s saw the emergence of the Fifth Generation of Chinese cinema. No prizes for guessing that the previous four, dating back to the silent era, had been largely ignored by the West (although a little state suppression here and there did the industry few favours, either). Zhang Yimou (*Raise the Red Lantern*, 1991) and Chen Kaige (*Farewell My Concubine*, 1993) are currently the most familiar names. However, pundits predict even greater things from the leading lights of the Sixth Generation.

None can match the global impact made by Hong Kong. While art-house devotees extol the virtues of Ann Hui and Wong Kar-wai, millions worldwide thrill to the 'chop-socky' and 'heroic bloodshed' flicks of the prolific action industry. In some areas, martial artists such as Bruce Lee, Jackie Chan and Chow Yun-fat are more famous than anything

Leslie Cheung in *Farewell My Concubine.* Although shot in China, the finance came from Hong Kong.

Bruce Lee in the Kung Fu action movie *Enter the Dragon* (1973).

Hollywood has to offer. But with several big-name directors like John Woo and Tsui Hark decamping to the States, it remains to be seen how this vibrant industry will fare under its new masters.

It's intriguing to speculate which previously neglected industry will catch the international imagination next – because, rest assured, one will.

1979 Bulgarian defector Georgi Markov is stabbed in the leg with a poisoned umbrella as he walks through London.

1981 The fairytale wedding of Charles, Prince of Wales, and Lady Diana Spencer takes place in St Paul's Cathedral.

1985 Compact discs and CD players are introduced. Music lovers have to jettison their albums and cassettes in the search for superior sound quality.

1970s to the present
Global Cinema
The English Speakers

If you thought Britain and America were two nations divided by a common language, what about Australia and the old country? Or New Zealand and Canada, for that matter?

Three schoolgirls and their teacher vanish in the Outback in *Picnic at Hanging Rock*.

A ustralian cinema had nabbed its place in the record books way back in 1906, when Charles Tait's *The Story of the Kelly Gang* became the first-ever feature film. But little more was heard from Down Under until the early 1970s when, demonstrating what a little state-funding can do, the Australian New Wave saw over 400 features produced in just over 15 years. The first film to make the world sit up and take notice was Peter Weir's *Picnic at Hanging Rock* (1975). A series of period pieces followed, including Bruce Beresford's *Breaker Morant* (1980) and Weir's *Gallipoli* (1981). Yet it was George Miller's *Mad Max* trilogy and the Paul Hogan vehicle, *Crocodile Dundee* (1986), that raked in the cash.

Things went a bit quiet after the big guns left for Hollywood (joined by New Zealanders Peter Jackson and Jane Campion). But Paul Cox and his ilk remained, forging respectable reputations without setting the world on fire. To many, Aussie cinema means ballroom dancers, drag queens and talking pigs, but an indie boom now looks set to change all that.

Canadian film folk are also prone to wanderlust. Since Ted Kotcheff's *The Apprenticeship of Duddy Kravitz* (1974) proved Canada capable of more than documentaries and cartoons, few have resisted the call of California. Yet art-house darling Atom Egoyan, horrormeister David Cronenberg and such Québecois directors as Denys Arcand have remained and prospered.

Mel Gibson became an international star and director after being discovered in the futuristic *Mad Max*.

1990 Garbo dies in the same year as Barbara Stanwyck, Sammy Davis Jr, Rex Harrison, Irene Dunne and Leonard Bernstein.

1993 Hubert Schwarz cycles round Australia (8,813 miles) in 42 days, 8 hours and 25 minutes.

1997 The population flees as a volcanic eruption destroys large areas of the island of Montserrat. Most of the island's buildings had been flattened by Hurricane Hugo in 1989.

Irish movies

Mention Irish cinema and you immediately think of films about the Troubles. But not every Irish movie is as focused on the political situation as Jim Sheridan's *In the Name of the Father* or Neil Jordan's *Michael Collins*. The conflict merely bookended Jordan's unique love story *The Crying Game*, while it barely merited a mention in the rites of passage pictures *Circle of Friends* and *The Last of the High Kings*. Ireland itself is also the star of many a Hollywood movie, notably standing in for Scotland in Mel Gibson's *Braveheart*.

hen he accepted his scar for *Chariots*, Colin elland proclaimed e British are coming!'

There are plenty of Brits leasing apartments in Tinseltown, too. The promise of credibility has resulted in onetime ad-directors and stage luvvies being snapped up by the studios for a fraction of the fees demanded by the Hollywood heavyweights.

For once, things look pretty rosy back in Blighty, too. Richard Attenborough and the Merchant-Ivory team have dominated the costume drama for over 25 years, although a more radical approach to literary adaptation has emerged in the late 1990s. There's even a healthy maverick strain, with Peter Greenaway following in the footsteps of Ken Russell and Derek Jarman.

British film revivals have invariably been boom-and-bust

Daniel Day Lewis and Gordon Warnecke are lovers in *My Beautiful Laundrette* (1985).

affairs. Bitter experience appears finally to have taught producers the folly of trying to compete, and co-operation now seems the only sensible policy. But this seemed a good idea in the 1930s and 1960s, too.

ROLL THE CREDITS

Although several Aussies and Brits have been lured to Tinseltown, few purchase one-way tickets. Directors **Gillian Armstrong** *and* **Fred Schepisi**, *as well as performers like* **Judy Davis** *and* **Sam Neill**, *regularly return Down Under. A whole troupe of British thesps, from* **Sean Connery** *and* **Michael Caine** *to* **Kenneth Branagh** *and* **Kate Winslet**, *have sampled the Hollywood limelight, but like directors* **Alan Parker** *and* **Ridley** *and* **Tony Scott**, *they've also got a stake in the British film revival.*

1969 Jack Kerouac dies. He was famous for coining the term the Beat Generation, which he explained as meaning 'beat down' or 'beatific'.

1970 Jimi Hendrix dies of a drug overdose in Paris. A left-hander, he was famous for playing a right-handed guitar upside-down.

1974 Europe's highest road is opened. The Pico de Veleta Pass in Sierra Nevada, Spain, is 11,384 feet above sea level.

1960s to the present

Highway 61 Revisited
Road Movies

Dennis Hopper and Peter Fonda as the hippie bikers in *Easy Rider*.

From the early days of the wagon trains and the westerns they inspired through to the classic Beat Generation novels like On The Road, *Americans have been obsessed with travelling the highways of their sprawling country. So it should be no surprise that the only truly original American genre was the road movie.*

But road movies are often much more than a glorified tourist trip. They examine not just the landscape of America, but also the country's values and social problems – as well as the developing characters of the travellers. Nicholas Ray's *They Live By Night* (1948) was typical of the genre, with escaped innocents on the run pursued by a corrupt and relentless police force. But it was the social divisions and tensions of the 1960s, together with

lighter cameras, making location shooting easier, that spawned the modern road movie. Dennis Hopper's seminal *Easy Rider* (1969) charted the surrealistic adventures of a pair of hippies who embark on a road trip and face prejudice and violence. As the poster tag line put it: 'A man went looking for America and couldn't find it anywhere!'

Terrence Malick's *Badlands* (1973) revealed another aspect of the road movie. His true story of a pair of youngsters (played by Martin Sheen and Sissy Spacek) who embark on a brutal and senseless killing spree delivered a nihilistic picture of disenfranchised youth and the violence and desperation that lurked beneath the surface of 'civilized' America. It was a

Badlands launched the careers of Sissy Spacek, Martin Sheen and director Terrence Malick.

1978 Superman, portrayed by Christopher Reeves, flies round the world in seconds and saves the universe.

1988 More than five million motorcycles are registered in the US.

1995 *The Usual Suspects* introduces mysterious master criminal Keyser Soze, but just who is he?

ROLL THE CREDITS

Peter Fonda *became an aficionado of the road movie, playing the 'wildest angel' in* **Roger Corman's** *movie about Hell's Angels in 1966 before he went on to co-write, produce and star in* Easy Rider *with* **Dennis Hopper.** *The latter launched the main-stream career of legendary hellraiser* **Jack Nicholson,** *who received an Oscar nomination for his role as the stoned lawyer.* **Dennis Hopper,** *one of the most chilling bad guys of the last decades, played the extortionist threatening to blow up the bus in* Speed *(1994).*

generate laughs from placing characters in racing situations across unfamiliar territories: *Mad Max* (1979) would take the genre into a posy apocalyptic future; Sam Peckinpah would adapt a country-and-western song and place the action in trucks in *Convoy* (1978); and *The Sure Thing* (1985) shoehorned the teen sex-comedy into the road movie genre. Even *The Wizard Of Oz* was effectively a musical road movie, albeit set in a Technicoloured fantasy land.

Partners in crime

'They are young, they are in love, they kill people.' The story of Depression-era gangsters Bonnie Parker and Clyde Barrow set a new trend for presenting criminals as sympathetic non-conformists. *Bonnie and Clyde* (1967) was extremely shocking in its day for the offhand way in which the young pair blast people to death but, influenced by the Nouvelle Vague, director Arthur Penn intercut the most tense episodes with lyrical love scenes set in beautiful MidWest countryside and events of almost slapstick comedy. The controversial ending set a new benchmark for violence on screen in 1967, but is tame compared to that in later partners-in-crime movies like *Natural Born Killers*. *Butch Cassidy and the Sundance Kid* paired Paul Newman and Robert Redford in 1969 and Ridley Scott introduced a new variation on the theme in 1991 when he cast Susan Sarandon and Geena Davis in *Thelma and Louise*, two women on a voyage of self-discovery, running away from the law and abusive men.

A feminist manifesto for the 1990s? Geena Davis and Susan Sarandon as *Thelma and Louise*.

theme that would be reflected in more recent films like *My Own Private Idaho* (1991), *Kalifornia* (1993) and Oliver Stone's ultra-violent satire *Natural Born Killers* (1994).

A less grim version of the road movie grew to brief prominence in the 1970s with chaotic chase films such as *Smokey And The Bandit* (1977), *The Cannonball Run* (1980) and *The Blues Brothers* (1980), which delivered spectacular car-stunts hung around gossamer-thin plots.

But the road movie is so embedded in American film culture that it has been reworked and incorporated into almost every other major genre. *Planes, Trains and Automobiles* (1987) and Martin Scorsese's *After Hours* (1985) are comedies that both use elements of the road movie to

1944 The Allies liberate Auschwitz and Belsen concentration camps.

1962 *West Side Story*, a musical updating of Shakespeare's Romeo and Juliet, wins ten Oscars.

1974 Elizabeth Taylor divorces Richard Burton for the first time and gets a settlement of $7.5 million plus the $5 million diamond he gave her.

1940s to the present
Mavericks
Welles and Kubrick

Until the day when making and distributing a film is as cheap and simple as writing a book, cinema will always involve some trade-off between artistic intent and commercial pressure. The vast majority of successful film directors manage to strike some sort of workable compromise between the colossal costs involved in producing a film and the purity of their own vision. Many, however, spend their artistic lives at loggerheads with their financial backers and earn the reputation as difficult, maverick figures.

Searching for Rosebud. Orson Welles as Citizen Kane.

Harrelson and Lewis, Stone's *Natural Born Killers* (1994).

Following in the footsteps of the silent era maverick, Erich von Stroheim, *Orson WELLES* (1915–1985) became Hollywood's premier *enfant terrible*. A precociously gifted child and an orphan by the age of 12, Welles combined a deep love of theatre with a happy knack for self-promotion, which won him a contract at RKO to direct his first feature. The result was *Citizen Kane* (1941), a milestone in modern cinema (although a commercial flop) which combined an innovative narrative structure with advances in the use of sound and revolutionary camerawork by Gregg Toland, to become what is now regularly garlanded as the greatest film of all time. Unsurprisingly, thereafter it proved downhill for 'Awesome

1980 Punk rock star Sid Vicious is found dead in a hotel room after a heroin overdose.

1985 Pop stars unite in the UK and US to produce Live Aid, a massive global concert to help famine victims in Africa.

1990 Margaret Thatcher cries while leaving Downing Street after colleagues vote her out of the longest-held British prime-ministership this century.

A Clockwork Orange

Upset by British tabloid claims that his movie had inspired a spate of gang attacks, Kubrick took the drastic step of banning it from British cinemas and video stores. Author Anthony Burgess hated the adaptation, which he thought corrupted his ironic futurist fable. When Alex, played by Malcolm McDowell, is released from prison, Burgess intended it to be a dark joke on the society onto which he's unleashed, but Kubrick made him seem like a heroic survivor of an oppressive regime, whose release we should cheer.

Alex is a sadist turned guinea pig.

Orson'. Welles fought innumerable battles with studio chiefs, who butchered most of his films, notably *The Magnificent Ambersons* (1942), and refused to finance or distribute them properly.

So too is *Stanley KUBRICK* (1928–1999), although here the parallels with Welles probably end. Hired as a replacement director on the epic *Spartacus* (1960), Kubrick swiftly earned a reputation for fastidious and fanatical attention to detail and followed that film's success with landmark films like *Dr Strangelove* (1963), *2001: A Space Odyssey* (1968) and *A Clockwork Orange* (1971).

The most romantic of the modern mavericks must be *Terrence MALICK* (1945–). Discouraged by the poor box office returns of *Badlands* (1973) and *Days Of Heaven* (1978), he went into early retirement, from which he has belatedly returned with the Second World War drama, *The Thin Red Line*.

Less liked, but probably the closest thing to a contemporary maverick is Vietnam veteran *Oliver STONE* (1946–), who relentlessly pursued controversy with *JFK* (1991), *Nixon* (1996) and *Natural Born Killers* (1994).

Keir Dullea searches for a Higher Power in *2001: A Space Odyssey*, outwitting the computer HAL.

ROLL THE CREDITS

Gregg Toland *was associated with a number of visually dramatic films besides* Citizen Kane. *He worked with* **Arthur Edeson** *on* All Quiet on the Western Front *(1930), made* **Peter Lorre** *look sinister in* Mad Love *(1935), photographed* **William Wyler's** Wuthering Heights *(1939) and* The Best Years of Our Lives *(1946) and* **John Ford's** The Grapes of Wrath *and* The Long Voyage Home *(1940).*

1968 Andy Warhol is shot and nearly killed by radical feminist Valerie Solanas.

1972 Lou Reed releases 'Walk on the Wild Side' from his album *Transformer*.

1980 Luis Alvarez controversially claims that the dinosaurs became extinct after a huge meteorite collided with the Earth.

1970s to the present

Paranoia and Parodies
Allen and Brooks

Of all the film genres hit by the increasing popularity of television, comedy was probably the most seriously wounded. Television was almost perfect for the intimacy in which comedy flourishes, and more importantly could deliver it in half-hour chunks. Thus the sit-com and sketch show became staples of TV schedules the world over, while comic movies, in general, declined both in quantity and originality. Thankfully, there were a few exceptions.

Allen as the robot servant in *Sleeper*.

Woody Allen, one of American film's true auteurs, started life as a stand-up comic and TV gag writer, but his early films *Take The Money And Run* (1969), and sci-fi satire, *Sleeper* (1972) demonstrated skills in almost every sphere of comedy, from spoof and wisecrack to slapstick. It was *Annie Hall* (1977), however, that really defined the Woody Allen style: blending nebbish one-liners and occasional tenderness against the backdrop of New York's upper-middle classes. *Manhattan* (1979) continued this

style, and apart from a few forays into 'serious' movie-making, with *Interiors* (1978), *Stardust Memories* (1980) and *Shadows and Fog* (1992) – all of which were as personal but generally less critically successful – he has continued that pattern.

Mel Brooks, too, started out as a TV gag writer; but that aside, he couldn't be more different. His first film, *The Producers* (1968), was instantly hailed as a comedy classic, but it was with *Blazing Saddles* (1974) that he established his style. The movie, an anarchic, surreal and rude spoof of the western, was typical of Brooks' subsequent films. *Young Frankenstein*

1986 The first Nintendo games appear in the US. Kids love helping the hero Link, who has to rescue Zelda.

1993 Hollywood explores the Holocaust, with Spielberg's film about Oskar Schindler, the German businessman who rescued more than a thousand Jews from the gas chambers.

1994 Carlos the Jackal is arrested in Damascus and brought to Paris for trial.

Woody Allen with frequent collaborator and one-time partner Diane Keaton in *Annie Hall*.

Saturday Night Live

It first went on air in 1975 and became one of TV's longest running shows, with its format of sketches, skits and songs. The late-night broadcast time meant they could feature irreverent, bawdy humour and it was responsible for launching the careers of countless comedians: Dan Ayckroyd, Bill Murray, Chevy Chase and John Belushi in the early years and, later on, Eddie Murphy, Joan Cusack and Mike Myers, whose *Wayne's World* began as a sketch on the show

produced *Airplane* (1980) and *The Naked Gun* (1988), continued the trend for genre spoofs. More recently, comedy appears to be in a downswing, although new talents include Mike Myers, who starred in *Wayne's World* (1992), *So I Married an Axe Murderer* (1993) and *Austin Powers* (1997). Jim Carrey's hectic, Jerry Lewis-inspired humour has delighted some (while irritating others). But for now, the biggest laughs seem to be on the small screen.

Mike Myers as *Austin Powers, International Man of Mystery*, set in the groovy 1960s.

(1974) and *High Anxiety* (1977) took hilarious swipes at horror and Hitchcock respectively. Zucker, Abrahams and Zucker, the writing and directing team that

Airplane (1980) is a massively successful lampoon of disaster movies.

ROLL THE CREDITS

Even if you had never seen him on screen, you could judge a lot about **Steve Martin** *from the titles of his movies* – The Jerk *(1979), in which he played the lead;* Dead Men Don't Wear Plaid *(1982) and* The Man With Two Brains *(1983), which were all directed by* **Carl Reiner**. *More versatile than his father,* **Rob Reiner** *has directed films as different as* When Harry Met Sally *(1989) and* Misery *(1990),* A Few Good Men *(1992) and the cult heavy metal spoof* This Is Spinal Tap *(1984).*

1985 Robert Greenburg imports Korean sneakers and sells them under the name LA Gear. Sales top $11 million in the first year and hit $224 million by 1988.

1992 Marlene Dietrich dies in Paris. Her last film role was opposite David Bowie in *Just a Gigolo* (1978).

1993 London's Planet Hollywood restaurant opens, backed by Bruce Willis and Sylvester Stallone.

1970s to the present

The New Hollywood
My People Will Call Your People

By the 1970s, the once mighty studio system lay in ruins. MGM, always the most powerful of the majors, had struggled on, but in 1969 the studio was bought and asset-stripped by millionaire hotelier Kirk Kerkorian; shortly afterwards it made its last film. The combined pressures of television, growing independent production and, most importantly of all the loss of the studios' theatre chains as a result of the Paramount Decrees all conspired to silence even MGM's roaring lion.

Cameron Diaz and Jim Carrey in *The Mask* (1994). He is known in the industry as 'Cash and Carrey'.

Lots on
the market.

What emerged during the next 20 years was a new machine for movie-making – a system based upon agents, publicists and packages, which, to some observers, has the sole aim of raising and raising again the fees asked by stars. Movies are produced not by studios but by massive conglomerates. 20th Century-Fox is part of Rupert Murdoch's News International corporation, which also owns newspapers, television stations and magazines across the world. The Coca Cola Company once owned Columbia Pictures before it was merged with Tri-Star to become Columbia Tri-Star, then bought by Japanese electronics giant

1994 An earthquake measuring 6.6 on the Richter scale hits Los Angeles. More than 60 are killed, thousands injured and 20,000 left homeless.

1998 Bill Clinton deftly fights accusations of sexual harassment and is the first president to testify in a court case while in office.

1998 The Oscars for Best Actor and Actress go to Jack Nicholson and Helen Hunt for *As Good as it Gets*.

Sony. But the talent – the stars, directors and crew – aren't 'owned' by the studios as they were in the golden age. They are all essentially freelancers, who through agents such as Creative Artists Agency and William Morris make deals (sometimes for a series of films) with these companies. In turn this gives a few top agencies (and agents) massive power to broker multi-million dollar deals for their clients, often providing not only the star of the movie, but also the co-stars and directors as part of a package.

The result has been spiralling pay for the top stars. It's not inconceivable that actors such as Tom Cruise, Jim Carrey and Arnold Schwarzenegger will soon demand fees as high as $30 million to appear in films, and also negotiate 'back end' deals in which they get a cut of the box office. In some cases, since this cut is considered as a cost, on paper at least some of the biggest box-office smashes never go into profit.

There seems to be no end to this upward pressure. And although studios often talk of trying to reduce the costs of making a film, inevitably movies like *Titanic* (1998) come along and leave studio heads waving their chequebooks in search of the next big production.

Titanic scooped a shelfload of Oscars and took over $1 billion at the box- office, earning back its $200 million production costs within weeks.

1975 The end of the much-hated Vietnam War. In the years from 1961 to 1975, 56,555 American soldiers are killed, one fifth of them by their own troops.

1978 More than 900 members of Jim Jones' People's Temple die in Jonestown, Guyana, after drinking a cocktail of powdered fruit juice and cyanide.

1979 A serious accident at the Three Mile Island nuclear power station in Pennsylvania occurs just before the release of *The China Syndrome* starring Jane Fonda, which features eerily similar events.

1970s to the present

From Angst to Escapism
Altman, Polanski and Spielberg

You can tell a lot about a nation's state of mind from the movies it goes to see. Just as horror had flourished in depression-stricken 1930s America, in the 1970s, the

Hoffman and Redford in *All the President's Men*.

atmosphere of national worry caused by the disastrous Vietnam War and Watergate was reflected in a plethora of downbeat, self-critical and ultimately disturbing films. But as the mood lightened with the economic recovery of the 1980s, cartoonish adventure and cute extra-terrestrials would be the order of the day.

Woman-chasing medics at a mobile army hospital in *M*A*S*H*.

Although Roman Polanski won great acclaim with his classic angst movie *Chinatown* (1974) – in which he slits Jack Nicholson's nose open – it was Robert Altman who was the chief auteur of the 1970s angst movies. His feature, *M*A*S*H* (1970), was a tragi-comic account of mobile army hospital life during the Korean War – blood-drenched, harrowing and hilarious in equal measure, and shot in Altman's soon-to-be trademark

documentary style. It alerted America to the horrors of war and to its own flippancy in refusing to examine them. His most famous and discussed movie is *Nashville* (1975). It has no discernible plot, but revolves around the lives of 24 characters in the eponymous country-and-western capital of America. For some critics, it is a razor-edged commentary on America's obsession with transient fame and its ability to ignore the darker aspects of the country and current events. The late 1970s were a fallow time for Altman and he wasn't to make amends until 1992, when his cameo-stuffed satire on Hollywood, *The Player*, as well as his ambitious and complex tale of six separate couples, *Short Cuts* (1993), restored his reputation.

Part of the reason for Altman's 1980s hiatus may have been the changing mood of the nation. America, now enjoying a

1987 An expedition led by Robert G. Ballard discovers the wreck of the Titanic.

1988 Pan Am flight PA103 blows up over Lockerbie in Scotland, killing the 259 people in the plane and 11 on the ground.

1993 River Phoenix collapses and dies outside his friend Johnny Depp's nightclub. He is only 22 and known as a vegetarian teetotaller, born to hippie parents in a log cabin in Oregon.

Liam Neeson negotiates with the Nazis to rescue Jews in *Schindler's List*.

boom and definitely less inclined to indulge in political and social self-criticism, was being enticed to the cinemas with light hearted, crowd-pleasing pieces such as *Close Encounters of the Third Kind* (1977), *E.T.* (1982), and *Raiders of the Lost Ark* (1984). The director of all three, Steven Spielberg, was about as far removed from the angst-ridden Altman as could be imagined. Interestingly, however, when America once again inclined toward self-examination, even Spielberg would begin to produce more serious and sober films, like *Schindler's List* (1993) and *Amistad* (1998).

ROLL THE CREDITS

Violence came to Hollywood in 1971 with movies like **William Friedkin's** The French Connection, **Don Siegel's** Dirty Harry, *and blaxploitation movie* Shaft *directed by* **Gordon Parks**. *Sex was also becoming much more explicit with* **Mike Nichols'** Carnal Knowledge *(1971) and* **Hal Ashby's** Shampoo *(1975).*

The conspiracy movie boomed with **Sydney Pollack's** Three Days of the Condor *(1975), and* The Parallax View *(1974) and* All the President's Men *(1976), both directed by* **Alan J. Pakula**.

Roman Polanski

It's little wonder that Polanski's films are infused with sexual tension, violence, obsession and alienation. He escaped from the Cracow ghetto through a hole in the wall and was shot at by German troops; his parents were shipped to concentration camps and his mother was gassed at Auschwitz; in 1969 his pregnant wife Sharon Tate was brutally murdered by a devil-worshipping gang led by Charles Manson; and in 1977 he had to flee the States, after allegations of sexual intercourse with a 13 year-old girl at Jack Nicholson's house.

Harrison Ford as Indiana Jones in *Raiders of the Lost Ark*, a stunt-packed action adventure.

1978 A great white shark weighing over 5,000lb and measuring over 20 feet long is harpooned by fishermen in the Azores.

1980 *Voyager I* reaches Saturn, and explores the planet's 14 moons and more than 1,000 rings. *Voyager* is on a 3-year journey of 1.3 billion miles.

1983 Ronald Reagan initiates a defence system that can zap his enemies from outer space, nicknamed Star Wars.

1970s to the present

Boom and Bust

Hollywood Blockbusters

A pilotless jet full of stars hurtles towards disaster in *Airport*.

The 1960s had been difficult for Hollywood. While it could boast some of the most original films of the period, with the likes of Bonnie and Clyde *(1967),* 2001: A Space Odyssey *(1968) and* The Wild Bunch *(1969), these movies were hardly the stuff that appealed to the mass-market the industry had been trying to woo since the collapse of the studio system. In the 1970s, Tinseltown rediscovered the art. It was the disaster movie that put bums back on seats.*

Airport (1970) was the first catastrophe flick to catch the public imagination. Like all the movies that followed, it presented a set of characters (a fair proportion of whom were obviously doomed) in some perilous situation, and invited the audience to watch them sink or swim. The movie was a massive success (making its $10 million budget back four times over) and throughout the decade the formula was repeated in increasingly spectacular and expensive fashion. *The Poseidon Adventure* (1972) was followed by *The Towering Inferno* (1974) and then came *The Hindenberg* (1975). The genre rapidly became one giant cliché, and was brilliantly spoofed in *Airplane* (1980), but the major effect it had was to drive the budgets of films relentlessly upwards. The trend spilled into other genres, and resulted in the birth of the modern blockbuster, movies where the sheer scale and expense of a film were presented as one of its big draws. *The Godfather* (1972), *Superman*

James Caan, Marlon Brando, Al Pacino and John Cazale in *The Godfather*.

1987 Condom commercials are shown on US television in an attempt to reverse the increase in cases of AIDS.

1991 Robert Maxwell dies in mysterious circumstances, falling from his yacht moored off the Canaries, and leaves millions of pounds worth of debt behind him.

1996 Scientists successfully clone a sheep called Dolly.

E.T.'s appearance remained a closely guarded secret until the film's release in 1982.

(1978) and *Star Trek: The Motion Picture* (1979) were all examples of how Hollywood thought that throwing money at a project could guarantee its success: between 1972 and 1979, the average cost of a feature almost quadrupled. Studios wagered their very existence on one or two films that had to open massively in order to make their money back. Then in 1980 United Artists was brought down by the box-office flop of *Heaven's Gate*, a western whose budget spiralled out of control. The studios declared the party over, and not until the 1990s would the same cycle of spending begin to repeat itself.

Ironically *Star Wars*, one of the most successful movies of all time, was made for just $12 million during this period and grossed over $300 million on release. It seemed that bigger wasn't always better after all...

ROLL THE CREDITS

In 1994 Dream Team director **Steven Spielberg**, *ex-Disney production executive* **Jeffrey Katzenburg** *and producer* **David Geffen** *got together to form the first new Hollywood studio in over sixty years called Dream Works SKG. Each invested an estimated $33.3 million, mere pocket money to them. They took over* **Howard Hughes**' *old airplane hangar and are supposed to be creating the most technologically advanced studio in Hollywood, despite the carping of their critics. The first Dreamworks movie,* The Peacemaker, *starring* **Nicole Kidman** *and* **George Clooney** *was released in 1997. A mix of live action and animated pictures is planned for the future.*

Alec Guinness battles Darth Vader in George Lucas's *Star Wars* (1977).

1972 Thirteen Roman Catholics are shot dead by British troops in Londonderry, on a day that comes to be known as Bloody Sunday.

1977 Two *Voyager* spacecraft explore the solar system. In case they meet aliens, each has a tape with 117 pictures of our planet, greetings in 54 languages, a selection of 'the sounds of Earth', and some of the world's music.

1979 France has the highest per capita alcohol consumption in the world, at around 17 quarts a year, but the police stop doing breathalizer tests after restaurateurs complain that it is harming business.

1970s to the present

The Movie Brats
Coppola, Scorsese and De Palma

'Men with beards': that is how the more mischievous film critics described the directorial troika of Martin Scorsese, Brian De Palma and Francis Ford Coppola. But these directors had more in common than just their facial hair: throughout the 1970s and 1980s they would each make modern classics. Whereas directors such as Hitchcock, Peckinpah and Hawks had learned the job by doing it, Scorsese, De Palma and Coppola had all graduated from film studies courses. The result was a much more knowing, technically adept, some would say over-polished style of film-making.

Apocalypse Now is a chaotic, visually spectacular adaptation of Joseph Conrad's *Heart of Darkness*.

Scorsese is noted for his ability to draw powerful performances from actors.

Francis Ford Coppola is best known for *Apocalypse Now* (1979) and *The Godfather* trilogy (1972, 1974 and 1990), a sprawling series of films that dramatized the lives and deaths of a Mafia family. He also dabbled in smaller-scale pictures (1983 teen-flicks *The Outsiders* and *Rumblefish*), but by the late 1980s seemed to have run out of creative steam.

Brian De Palma has had a career characterized by brilliant ups and disastrous downs (like *Bonfire of the Vanities*, 1990). Often, and to his irritation, compared to Hitchcock, he is the most determinedly commercial of the movie brats. Early horror films such as *Carrie* (1976) and *The Fury* (1978) revealed his talent for technically dazzling set pieces. But with *Body Double* (1984), a porn-themed thriller, he would attract accusations of sensationalism and misogyny. The patchiness of his work has led many critics to dismiss him as a talented hack, but he is undoubtedly

1987 Oliver Stone's *Platoon* starts a new fashion for Vietnam movies, seven years after *Apocalypse Now*.

1995 The trial of O.J. Simpson for the murder of his wife Nicole grips the American public. An average of 5.5 million people watch it every day on television.

1996 Hollywood Madame Heidi Fleiss is arrested and promises to name names.

ROLL THE CREDITS

Paul Schrader's *screenwriting credits include several for Scorsese* – Taxi Driver *(1976)*, Raging Bull *(1980) and* The Last Temptation of Christ *(1988). He also proved himself a capable director with* Blue Collar *(1978) and* Mishima: A Life in Four Chapters *(1985).*

Innocence (1993). Scorsese, a vastly knowledgeable cinephile, is technically highly skilled and masterful in his use of contemporary music, and he has had few critical failures.

All three directors paved the way for a new generation of film-makers – Quentin Tarantino amongst them – for whom a knowledge of the technology and history of their medium was as important as a good story.

capable of producing disturbing and inventive films such as *Casualties of War* (1989) and *Carlito's Way* (1993), plus blockbusters to order, as he proved with *Mission: Impossible* (1996).

But if one of the three has been consistently fascinating, it is Martin Scorsese. His films, from the early *Mean Streets* (1973) and *Taxi Driver* (1976), established his frequent collaboration with Robert De Niro and his fascination with gangsters, street life and accounts of moral corruption and psychological collapse. *Raging Bull* (1980), *The King of Comedy* (1983) and *Good Fellas* (1990) would continue this relationship and theme; but Scorsese also tackled a couple of unusual subjects with *The Last Temptation of Christ* (1988) and costume drama *The Age of*

Scorsese's outstanding feature tells of young men growing up in Manhattan's Little Italy.

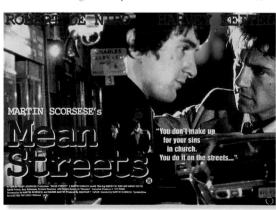

1974 Uri Geller mends watches and bends spoons using extrasensory powers.

1977 Stephen King writes *The Shining*; the movie version casts Jack Nicholson as a grinning homicidal maniac.

1980 Roller blades are first produced by 20-year-old Canadian hockey player Scott Olsen and his 16-year-old brother Brennan.

1974~Present

Teens and Terror
Slashers and College Kids

After the first flourishes of the teenpic in the 1950s and 1960s, cinema showed no intention of slackening its grip on young pockets or imaginations in succeeding decades. Teenage appetite for cinema that reflected adolescent lives and interests was a constant, and the studios were eager to capitalize on the spare money and leisure time of the younger generation. Oddly enough, the movies that resulted during the 1970s and 1980s were of two kinds: those that celebrated the mores of the average suburban kid, and those that depicted the very same teens being bloodily despatched to the Almighty.

John Hughes was the king of the 1980s teen-flick. With films like *Sixteen Candles* (1984), *Pretty In Pink* (1986) and *The Breakfast Club* (1985), he tapped directly in to the hopes, dreams and anxieties of the average American brat. Introducing a number of talented unknowns, such as Emilio Estevez and Molly Ringwald, he fed his grateful audience the message that their lives were as relevant, funny and dramatic as their parents'. Possibly his greatest creation was *Ferris Bueller's Day Off* (1986), a charming, exuberant romp through the possibilities offered to the eponymous hero (played by Matthew Broderick) by virtue of his being young and American in the 1980s. The British industry dabbled in the genre but in typically twee style, with films like *Gregory's Girl* (1980).

Copycats?

Virtually since the birth of the movies, moral watchdogs have claimed that films corrupt youth and inspire the deranged. The Production Code largely kept film-makers in check, but since the late 60s, there has been a marked increase in screen violence. But there's no concrete proof that brutal films have anything to do with rising crime rates. In 1973, Stanley Kubrick withdrew *A Clockwork Orange* from British distribution rather than have the tabloids blame it for a spate of sadistic assaults. Similarly, Oliver Stone's *Natural Born Killers* was cited as the inspiration for copycat killings in France and the US, but many believe the film was merely a convenient scapegoat for society's failure.

Judd Nelson, Emilio Estevez, Ally Sheedy, Molly Ringwald and Anthony-Michael Hall are classmates in *The Breakfast Club*.

1982 Michael Jackson's *Thriller* is the most popular album of all time, with 47 million copies sold.

1989 Chinese students demonstrate in Tiananmen Square; soldiers with AK47 rifles kill hundreds and the world's media film a lone protester trying to stop a tank.

1992 Disney's *Aladdin* features Robin Williams as the voice of the Genie.

In *Nightmare on Elm Street*, Robert Englund plays Freddy Krueger, a child murderer who burned to death fleeing the law and has now returned to haunt his old neighbourhood.

The teen movie's darker side had erupted in the 1970s. Brian De Palma's *Carrie* blended high-school drama with blood-soaked horror in 1976, but it was John Carpenter's *Halloween* (1978), a masterful shocker about young people murdered and terrorized by a faceless bogeyman, that launched an avalanche of mostly inferior imitations. The world can thank Wes Craven's *A Nightmare on Elm Street* (1984) for engendering the horribly scarred child-molester Freddy Krueger, whose dream-stalking resulted in countless sleepless nights. One of the most infamous of the 1970s schlockers was *The Texas Chainsaw Massacre* (1974), made on a shoestring by Tobe Hooper. The film was (many thought wrongly) identified as a 'video nasty' and banned by the British Government.

The teen-slasher was the success story of the 1980s, with a full 60 per cent of Hollywood's 1981 output devoted to this kind of American nightmare movie. But with the 1990s, it began to show its age. Rites of passage dramas were replaced by the 'slacker' movie: films about older college kids who found little to get excited about in modern life. The horror movie seemed in terminal decline until Wes Craven deconstructed the formula with the knowing spoof *Scream* (1997), and proved there was life in the old genre yet.

ROLL THE CREDITS

'The Brat Pack' was the collective term used to describe those who appeared in the 1985 movie St Elmo's Fire, *and is universally detested by its members. With the exception of* **Demi Moore**, *few of the 80s Brat Pack were still opening movies in the 1990s. Yet several of the decade's other young stars have prospered, notably* **Tom Cruise** *and* **Nicolas Cage**. **Sean Penn** *has emerged from the temperamental Mrs Madonna tag to become a fine character actor. But life's not been so good for those other 80s bad boys,* **Rob Lowe** *and* **Charlie Sheen**, *whose off-screen activities have made more headlines than their careers.*

1967 Arnold Schwarzenegger becomes Mr Universe. He wins that title five times, and becomes Mr Olympia seven times before retiring to work in film.

1975–9 Pol Pot's regime causes the death of more than 1 million Cambodians.

1980 Middle rank film star Ronald Reagan is elected 40th president of the United States.

1960s to the present
Make My Day
The Action Men

Hollywood has always had heroes – men willing to take enormous risks and perform daring stunts all for the love of country and, preferably, a good woman. The first of the modern action men was James Bond, played since his first incarnation in Dr No *(1962) by no fewer than six actors – Sean Connery, David Niven, George Lazenby, Roger Moore, Timothy Dalton and Pierce Brosnan. The series has even survived the death of its creator, Cubby Broccoli, with* Tomorrow Never Dies *(1997).*

The Bond formula: a promiscuous secret agent, buxom beauties, corny gags and evil villains.

Clint Eastwood, however, usually plays a very different action hero from Bond. He came to prominence as the enigmatic 'man with no name' in the stylish spaghetti westerns of Sergio Leone. In the 1970s he took the same kind of vigilante attitude and placed it against the backdrop of contemporary San Francisco as Detective 'Dirty' Harry Callaghan. In *Dirty Harry* (1971) and its sequels – including *Magnum Force* (1973) and *The Enforcer* (1976) – Eastwood would play a cop willing to break the law in order to save justice, while delivering stylish one-liners (including the infamous 'Do you feel lucky, punk?' speech). Now in his late sixties, he continues to make films, of which *In The Line Of Fire* (1993), a wry

look at an ageing FBI agent, is is a worthy example.

Sylvester Stallone and Arnold Schwarzenegger typified the cartoonish action hero of the 1980s. Ultra-violent movies such as *Rambo* (1985) and *Predator* (1987) presented their muscular heroes engaging in implausible adventures, in the case of Rambo rescuing POWs from Vietnam. The movies boasted bodycounts in the hundreds, spectacular firefights and virtually no plot. Eventually they were attacked for their crass xenophobia and for their glorification of bloody violence.

Clint Eastwood confirmed his cult status as Harry Callahan in a series of rogue cop movies starting with *Dirty Harry* (1971).

Break a leg!

With the size of the budgets and stars' fees on these movies, the insurance companies aren't keen on them being driven across the lot without a seatbelt on, never mind doing their own stunts. The first movie stuntman, Frank Hanaway, fell off a horse in *The Great Train Robbery* (1903) and the first stuntwoman, Helen Gibson, appeared in *The Hazards of Helen* (1914). A.J. Bakunus jumped 232 feet without a parachute, doubling for Burt Reynolds in *Hooper* (1978). Dar Robinson did a free-fall of 1,100 feet, opening his parachute just 300 feet from the ground for *Highpoint*, and earned $150,000 for his efforts. And in *Smokey and the Bandit II*, Gary Davis leapt 163 feet in a car, after accelerating up a ramp, reaching 80 miles per hour. Some stars insist on doing their own stunts, though, and Harrison Ford was nearly killed by the blades of a ship's propeller during the shooting of *Indiana Jones and the Last Crusade*.

Renny Harlin, an expert at the high-octane actioner, directed Bruce Willis in *Die Hard 2: Die Harder* (1990).

A new kind of hero was needed, and arrived in the form of Bruce Willis in *Die Hard* (1988), in which the over-pumped superhero was exchanged for an ordinary guy forced to perform acts of heroism. Wit and intelligence replaced the racism and cruelty, but the action was no less spectacularly staged.

The trend towards smarter action movies reached its zenith in 1997 with John Woo's *Face/Off*, a knowing, ironic take on the genre with John Travolta and Nicolas Cage exchanging visages. Whether this kind of film will be able to resist dumbing down again remains to be seen.

Stallone starred in a porn film before hitting pay dirt with *Rocky* (1976) and then *Rambo* (right).

ROLL THE CREDITS

Jean-Claude Van Damme *(the muscles from Brussels) and Swedish hunk* **Dolph Lungren** *were paired in* Universal Soldier *(1992) in which they played zombie warriors. Previously a marshal arts instructor,* **Stephen Seagal** *took to violent action movies like a duck to water in such classics as* Under Siege *(1986). Action villains are invariably played by Brits –* **Alan Rickman** *in* Die Hard, **Jeremy Irons** *in* Die Hard with a Vengeance *and* **Gary Oldman** *in* Air Force One.

1980 The US government declares it illegal to introduce a virus to someone else's computer.

1982 The first artifical hearts are transplanted into humans, but it soon transpires they don't work very well.

1988 Who Framed Roger Rabbit? is the first film to combine cartoon characters and live action. It stars Bob Hoskins alongside Roger and Jessica Rabbit.

1980s to the present

Hasta La Vista, Baby
Event Movies

The image of the White House exploding in *Independence Day's* trailer was much-talked-about.

All of cinema is basically a special effect. The principle of persistence of vision is used to fool the eye into thinking that a string of still images are one moving one. So it should be no surprise that special effects have proved to be major ingredients in films as diverse as San Francisco *(1936),* Forbidden Planet *(1956),* 2001: A Space Odyssey *(1968) or* Forrest Gump *(1994). In the 1980s, however, the effects began to be the main draw of a kind of megabudget blockbuster, termed by the industry as 'event movies'. Everything about an event movie is big, preferably bigger than the one released only a few months ago. The star's salary, the special effects budget, the volume of the soundtrack and the amount of time, effort and money put into the marketing campaigns behind them are all constantly spiralling upwards.*

The first of the modern event directors was probably Steven Spielberg, but his family-friendly films were soon accompanied by new, more adult-orientated fare. John McTiernan and Renny Harlin directed the three *Die Hard* movies, each costing and making more than the last. Another key name in this category is Roland Emmerich, whose *Independence Day* (1996) boasted ground-breaking Computer Generated Imagery (CGI) and was a box-office smash, not least because of the masterful way in which it was marketed. A teaser trailer was shown

a full year before the movie and its release was hotly anticipated. Spielberg himself would return to the fray with *Jurassic Park* (1993) and *Lost World: Jurassic Park* (1997), using the same technology to produce terrifyingly realistic dinosaurs.

But it is James Cameron who, in the 1990s, became the master of the event movie. Although his original *Terminator* (1984) had been a low-budget success, his sequel, *Terminator 2: Judgement Day* (1991) smashed budget records ($98 million) and confirmed star Arnold Schwarzenegger as one of the most

1989 A computer is developed at Carnegie Mellon University with a voice-recognition programme that has a vocabulary of 1,000 words.

1992 One in two marriages in the US ends in divorce. There are 2.4 million marriages this year and 1.2 million divorces.

1997 Members of several sects worldwide commit suicide in the belief that their souls will travel to eternity on the back of the Hale-Bopp comet.

successful of all time. *Aliens* (1986), his sequel to Ridley Scott's *Alien* (1979), took another medium-budget film and gave it the blockbuster treatment, while *Titanic* (1998) took budgets and box-office returns to a new peak. However, there are signs that Hollywood may be getting worried. In 1998, *Crusades* and *Superman Reborn*, both with projected budgets of over $100 million, were put on hold by the studios, perhaps mindful of the potentially catastrophic financial consequences of a dud blockbuster.

Sigourney Weaver plays Ripley, stubbornly fighting off drooling monsters in *Aliens*.

Merchandising

Cashing in on the movies is nothing new – there were Charlie Chaplin and Shirley Temple dolls back in the 1920s and 1930s. The most successful movie so far for lucrative merchandising is Warner Bros.' *Batman* (1989). Warners issued more than 160 licences to produce Batmen, Batmobiles, Jokers, and assorted Bat-gear, adding an estimated $50 million in earnings to the box-office receipts. All the kids' movies do it now: as well as models, fans can collect the T-shirts, mugs, books, badges, posters, duvets, ashtrays, mouse mats and boxer shorts tied in to their favourites and help make the big studios just a little bit richer.

ROLL THE CREDITS

The Australian movie Mad Max *(1979) starring* **Mel Gibson** *cost $350,000 to make and grossed $100 million in its first two years. Nicknamed 'Fishtar' after the disastrous* **Warren Beatty** *vehicle* Ishtar, **Kevin Costner's** Waterworld *(1995) cost an estimated $160 million and was tipped to sink without trace. But they said that about* Titanic. **Spielberg's** Jurassic Park *made over $100 million at the box-office within 9½ days of its release;* Emmerich's Independence Day *took just 6½ days, and* The Lost World: Jurassic Park *passed the $100 million mark in 5½ days. On the other hand,* Cutthroat Island, *directed by Renny Harlin, cost over $100 million to produce and within a year of its release had earned back an estimated $11 million. But the biggest budget-to-box-office flop is* Orphans *(1987), which cost $15 million and made $0.1 million.*

Schwarzenegger plays the cyborg assassin who's come back from the future in *Terminator 2*.

1982 E-mail via fax machines cuts transmission time down to 20 seconds a page, compared to 6 minutes on the very first models.

1988 Three giant turtles weighing 22kg (50lb) each are found in New York's sewage system.

1991 The Supreme Court rules that states are allowed to ban nude dancing and insist on g-strings being worn.

1980s to the present

Indie Cinema
New American Auteurs

American 'indie' cinema has become more and more admired, influential and – strangely enough – profitable, with all the major production companies starting up 'independent' wings. Which of course makes it difficult to say what an independent film truly is. Perhaps it is better to talk about independent film-makers: directors who refuse to compromise their visions, and make films irrespective of either the studio formulas for hits or the immediate profitability. These are the new American auteurs.

ROLL THE CREDITS

The godfather of American indie cinema was **John Cassavetes** *(1929–89), who broke the Hollywood mould with low-budget, improvized dramas like* Faces *(1968) and* Husbands *(1970). Several European directors have inspired the independents, most notably Finland's* **Aki Kaurismäki**, *whose* Leningrad Cowboys Go America *(1989) was an offbeat reworking of the road movie. With a talent for cameos that knows no bounds,* **Steve Buscemi** *has become an indie icon in roles like Mr Pink in* Reservoir Dogs *and the hit man in the Coen brothers'* Fargo, *which won Joel's wife* **Frances McDormand** *an Oscar as the unflappable, pregnant sheriff.*

Jim Jarmusch, one of the key independent film-makers of the 1980s, made his debut with *Permanent Vacation*

Uma Thurman in *Pulp Fiction.*

(1981) before delivering *Stranger Than Paradise* (1984), a quirky, almost plotless comedy which offered stunning black-and-white photography and an acute sense of style. But it was *Mystery Train* (1989) and *Night On Earth* (1992), a whimsical anthology of stories about five characters who take simultaneous taxi rides in five cities around the world, that brought him to greater public view and wider critical acclaim.

Hal Hartley's debut feature, *The Unbelievable Truth* (1990), made on a budget raised from bank loans, established him as a leading and idiosyncratic film-maker whose focus on eccentric but touching characters would be demonstrated with *Trust* (1991), *Simple Men* (1992) and particularly *Amateur* (1994), which deals with an amnesiac who meets an ex-nun making a living as a pornographer.

1992 Spike Lee's movie *Malcolm X* includes videotape footage of the Los Angeles police beating up Rodney King, an event that sparked riots earlier in the year.

1994 Derek Jarman dies of AIDS. His last film *Blue* is a spoken commentary about the progress of the disease over a bright blue background.

1996 Scientists warn that a deadly brain disease in humans could be caused by eating beef from mad cows.

Nicolas Cage and Holly Hunter in *Raising Arizona*, the Coen brothers concept of a screwball comedy.

Joel and Ethan Coen, a sibling directing and writing team, have managed to launch themselves as immensely commercially successful film-makers while retaining their independent, off-beat roots. *Blood Simple* (1984) was a stylish neo-noir thriller, while *Raising Arizona* (1987) was an unconventional take on the screwball comedy, with Nicolas Cage and Holly Hunter as a couple intent on abducting a baby. With more recent movies such as *The Hudsucker Proxy* (1994), the Oscar-winning *Fargo* (1995) and *The Big Lebowski* (1998), their films have become increasingly ambitious and popular without losing the dark

humour that has become their trademark. In the 1990s, a new generation of independent film-makers grew up, many of them capitalizing on the 'slacker' genre: movies based on aimless, over-educated young people in dull jobs, and taking advantage of the falling cost of equipment. Richard Linklater would make *Slacker* (1991), a strange look at a day in the lives of the misfits of Austin, Texas; and *Dazed And Confused* (1993), which follows a bewildered set of high-school kids as they graduate. Kevin Smith, in similar vein, would make *Clerks* (1994), a hilarious glimpse of life at a convenience store, filmed on a minuscule budget. Both directors would go on to make larger budget films while managing to retain the whimsical 'goof-off' nature of their film-making.

The Cult of Quentin

Just as the directors of the Nouvelle Vague were the first cine-literate film-makers, Quentin Tarantino is the first video geek made good. After hours in front of a goggle box screening everything from sitcoms to art-house, the former video store assistant now drops pop culture references into his movies with the nonchalance of Godard. Taking 1990s cinema by the scruff of the neck with *Reservoir Dogs* (1992), he gained respectability with the Cannes-winning *Pulp Fiction* (1994). In true maverick style, he spent the next three years cameoing in other people's movies, before wielding the megaphone once more for *Jackie Brown* (1997).

Isabelle Huppert always chooses quality roles. Here she plays the ex-nun in *Amateur*.

127

1977 The Sex Pistols release their notorious and much-banned single 'God Save the Queen' from the album *Never Mind the Bollocks*.

1983 Alice Walker writes *The Color Purple*. Whoopi Goldberg and Oprah Winfrey would star in the film version.

1989 Mel Blanc, 'the man of 1,000 voices' dies. In a 60-year career, he was responsible for the voices of Tweetie Pie, Daffy Duck, Sylvester, Speedy Gonzales, Woody Woodpecker, Barney Rubble and Bugs Bunny.

1970s to the present

Breaking the Mould
Who Says All Directors Are White Men?

Like virtually every other industry, Hollywood movie-making has been dominated until very recently by white males. While there have been a few exceptions over the years – African American Oscar Micheaux broke through in the 1920s, and Dorothy Arzner became a successful director in the 1930s and 1940s – Hollywood seems to have been a segregated boys' club. But as society changed during the 1960s and 1970s those so far excluded took at least faltering steps towards making their mark.

Barbra Streisand, in costume for her own screen role, directs the action of *Yentl*.

Melvin Van Peebles is one of the most significant black directors of the 1970s. His *Sweet Sweetback's Baadasss Song* (1970) was aimed specifically at an urban black audience tired of seeing either patronizing or outright offensive depictions of themselves. Its success opened the way for the 'blaxploitation' movies. Often loaded with violence and sex, these films were immensely popular with their intended audience. Some became cult items, amongst them *Shaft* (1971), *Super-Fly* (1972) and even *Blacula* (1972) – as the title suggests, a black take on the horror classic. In general, however, blaxploitation movies were of marginal interest to the main-stream cinemagoer. Eventually the characters became clichés, the fad waned and it seemed as though

black directors would again find themselves struggling to make films.

But in the late 1980s Spike Lee thundered onto the movie scene with *She's Gotta Have It* (1986), a micro-budget comedy which, through critical raves, put black film-making at least partially on the map. Commercial successes like *School Daze* (1988) and *Do The Right Thing* (1989), a controversial, violent and emotional slice of ethnic life, resulted in Lee being considered one of America's most interesting

Denzel Washington plays Malcolm X in Spike Lee's 1992 movie.

1993 26.6 million Americans (a tenth of the population) rely on food stamps to help them get enough to eat.

1995 Allied forces evict Saddam Hussein's troops from Kuwait in Operation Desert Storm.

1997 Mike Tyson bites a chunk from the ear of Evander Holyfield during a world title fight.

directors – of any colour. The biopic *Malcolm X* (1992) was criticized by some for taking liberties with the truth, but remains the most ambitious film directed by a black man in Hollywood history.

Women have had an equally difficult time in Hollywood. But there are, thankfully, exceptions. Barbra Streisand has been one of the most successful female directors, with her films *Yentl* (1983) and *The Prince Of Tides* (1991) widely praised. Penelope Spheeris and Amy Heckerling

have scored with comedies such as *Wayne's World* (1992) and *Fast Times At Ridgemont High* (1982) respectively, while Kathryn Bigelow even took on that most macho of genres, the action movie, with *Point Break* (1991) and *Strange Days* (1995). New Zealander Jane Campion triumphed at Cannes with *The Piano* (1993).

Yet even now, Hollywood remains a tough industry to break into, both for women and for ethnic minorities.

New Queer Cinema

There have been veiled references to the love that dare not speak its name since the early silent era. But it is only in the last quarter of the 20th-century that gay issues have been tackled openly on screen. Britain's Derek Jarman broke many taboos in films like *Sebastiane* (1976), which also happened to be the first feature made in Latin. Gay and lesbian pictures tend to come from the indie sector. But soon Hollywood spotted this untapped market, although it shied away from the more aggressive attitudes of New Queer Cinema by putting a typically melodramatic gloss on topics like AIDS in *Philadelphia* (1993).

ROLL THE CREDITS

The LAPD were on standby for potential riots at the opening of **John Singleton's** *directorial debut* Boyz N the Hood *(1991), which painted an uncompromising picture of life on the streets in South Central LA. The* **Hughes brothers,** *Allen and Albert, have continued this style of angry protest with abrasive pictures like* Dead Presidents *(1995). While most black directors operate on the indie circuit, several women film-makers work within the Hollywood system. After seven years in the sitcom* Laverne and Shirley, **Penny Marshall** *made her name as a director with* Big *(1988), while* **Betty Thomas** *was a regular on* Hill Street Blues *before helming comedies as different as* The Brady Bunch Movie *(1995) and* Private Parts *(1996).*

Anna Paquin and Holly Hunter appeared with Sam Neill and Harvey Keitel in *The Piano*.

1990 Macauley Culkin is left *Home Alone*. He starts a new trend for child stars but his own career proves short, though lucrative.

1994 Damien HIrst displays a shark in formaldehyde at the Tate Gallery.

1995 Deep Blue is the first computer to beat a human chess grandmaster, when it triumphs over Gary Kasparov in Philadelphia.

2000 and beyond

Coming Soon

The Technology of Tomorrow

When is a film not a film? When it's been shot on HDV and shown via DBS. So, farewell then, celluloid? Not quite. Video still can't duplicate

the richness and fidelity of film colour. However, it's far cheaper, and much more user-friendly for special-effects artists. The move to high-definition video is already gaining pace but, mercifully, 'theatre television' is still some way off. In a DBS world, projectors would be obsolete and movies would be broadcast direct to the big screen via satellite. It would save a bundle on distribution costs, but would it still be cinema? The writing's been on the wall for film as we know it for quite some time.

HDV arrived on the scene with *Julia and Julia* in 1987.

The Czech Laterna Magika system offered the tantalizing prospect of interactive movies as early as 1958. A decade later, IMAX began presenting films ten times bigger than the norm, while OMNIMAX promised a 165° wraparound image that placed the viewer at the very heart of the action. In the 1990s, IMAX launched a 3-D process, in which the audience watches the action through liquid crystal headsets.

Not every technological advance merited a seal of approval, however. Launched in 1984, 'colorization' enabled technicians without an artistic bone in their bodies to add colour electronically to black-and-

Toy Story (1995) was the first entirely computerized feature film.

1996 Oasis dominates the UK pop scene with nine singles spending 134 weeks in the charts over the course of the year.

1997 Madonna provokes condemnation from the Catholic church after calling her baby Lourdes.

1998 Bill Gates, head of Microsoft, is pelted with custard pies in Belgium for allegedly taking himself too seriously.

3-D computer effects debuted in *Futureworld* (1974).

ROLL THE CREDITS

Founded by **George Lucas**, *Industrial Light & Magic has long been at the sharp end of movie technology. One of its old boys,* **John Dykstra** *won an Oscar for his invention of the computer-controlled Dykstraflex camera. Another of his former bosses,* **Douglas Trumbull**, *is the grand old man of widescreen. The inventor of the giant Showscan system has also worked with IMAX on producing the ultimate viewing experience. Although* **Alex Jacobson** *and* **Victor Evtukov** *produced moving holographic images of an aquarium back in 1969, the hologram movie is still some way away. The lasers required to create the pictures are too dangerous to risk human subjects, let alone major movie stars.*

white images. Distorting the vision of the original director and perverting the course of movie history, these monstrosities proved depressingly popular with audiences, although critics and film-makers detested them.

Adverts
Advertising execs have been using reworked film footage for some time now, so that Humphrey Bogart appears to endorse a particular brand of beer and Steve McQueen races round mountain passes in a brand-new state-of-the-art sports car. Next they'll have Garbo doing condom commercials and Bela Lugosi selling dental floss.

On the home entertainment front, Sony and JVC began their short-lived video war in the mid-1970s (hands up all those who bought Betamax). Philips launched CD-i in the early 1990s, dangling the possibility of altering the ending of films like *Gone with the Wind*, or even appearing in them yourself. By the turn of the millennium, there was even talk of new roles for long-dead icons and permanent youth for the stars of today via digital recreation.

By 1995, stars like Mark Hamill and Dennis Hopper were appearing in CD-ROM games and boffins were talking up the possibility of fully interactive virtual reality cinema.

Although it's postponed their introduction, Hollywood has rarely resisted new technologies. Some sort of movie revolution is in the offing, but whether it will lead to a division into theme-park and art-house remains to be seen.

Roll the Credits

Featuring all the people we would like to thank for making all these movies possible.

PRODUCER

The individual who commissions the script, raises the budget, hires the director, complains about schedules and gets nominated for Best Picture Oscars.

EXECUTIVE PRODUCER

Someone appointed by the studio or production company to oversee the business aspects of a movie and/or supervise the producer. The credit is often given to anyone who's helped raise the budget.

DIRECTOR

The person who calls the shots and yeas or nays everything that goes before the camera.

SCREENWRITER

The author of the script, working either from an original story or an existing source. Often the director him/herself.

CASTING DIRECTOR

The person who selects and hires the cast. Nowadays the headline stars are attached to a package at the outset and casting directors principally handle the supporting and minor roles.

ART DIRECTOR

The production designer establishes the visual quality and atmosphere of a film via its sets, props and costumes.

STORYBOARD ARTIST

An illustrator who sketches the content of each shot to provide a rough outline of the film's storyline or continuity.

SET DECORATOR

The person who dresses a film set with the props and furnishings requested by the art director.

COSTUME DESIGNER

The individual who researches the historical or social context of a film and designs the costumes accordingly.

MAKE-UP ARTIST

The person who designs and applies the make-up, from the simplest cosmetics to the most complex special effects.

SECOND-UNIT DIRECTOR

The director who not only shoots incidental location scenes, but also stages large-scale action sequences involving extras, vehicles, animals, etc.

EXTRA

An uncredited performer used in non-speaking incidental roles or crowd scenes.

STAND-IN

An uncredited performer physically resembling the star who doubles for them on the set during lighting and camera tests, and occasionally on location or second-unit shoots. This includes body doubles, like the one that stood in for Kevin Costner in the scene where he had to bare his bottom in *Dances With Wolves*.

STUNT PERFORMERS

Stand-ins who undertake action or stunts considered too dangerous for the stars.

CINEMATOGRAPHER

The director of photography, who commands the camera crew and decides how scenes are to be lit.

MATTE ARTIST

The person who designs and paints the background scenery required for special effects or matte shots – e.g. vistas from long ago or in the distant future.

CAMERA OPERATOR

The person responsible for operating the camera during a take, in accordance with the orders of the director and cinematographer.

CLAPPER/LOADER

The individual responsible for loading film into the camera and holding the clapperboard in front of the lens before the action starts, to identify each take.

FOCUS PULLER

The member of the camera crew who adjusts the lens during a take to ensure the action remains in focus.

GAFFER

The chief electrician, who, under the supervision of the cinematographer, positions and maintains the lighting during shooting.

BEST BOY

The gaffer's chief assistant.

GRIPS

The film equivalent of a stagehand. Grips are responsible for moving the camera around on cranes and dollies (see crib sheet); they also lay the dolly tracks, position light reflectors and help shift scenery. The head of the crew is the key grip.

SCRIPT SUPERVISOR

An assistant to the director who notes any changes in the dialogue and the positions of performers and props at the end of a take to ensure perfect continuity between shots.

SOUND RECORDIST

The person who records the dialogue and background sound during studio and location shooting.

BOOM OPERATOR

The individual who holds the long pole or boom carrying the microphone above the actors during a take.

EDITOR

The individual who uses their technical, dramatic and artistic judgement to assemble the different shots into an order that determines the tempo, emphasis and impact of the action.

SPECIAL EFFECTS ARTIST

A specialist in creating visual effects. Some SFX are created with models and miniatures, optical processes or computer animation, while physical effects are achieved with make-up, paintings, stunt apparatus, and fire, water and weather machinery.

FOLEY ARTIST

A sound effects specialist who performs such incidental noises as footsteps, punches, kisses and door slams.

COMPOSER

The person who writes the musical score heard during a film.

SOUND EDITOR

The technician responsible for mixing together the dialogue, the score and sound effects into a single soundtrack.

TITLE DESIGNER

The artist who designs the graphics and images used in a film's opening credit sequence.

UNIT PUBLICIST

A PR specialist who secures media exposure for a film and arranges for it to be seen by critics.

Directors' Cut

A name-dropper's guide to 25 acclaimed directors from around the world. Don't go to the arthouse without it.

CHANTAL AKERMAN (B.1950) BELGIAN.
Brings an avant-garde background into features invariably focusing on the concerns of women in the modern world, most notably *Jeanne Dielman, 23 quai du Commerce, 1080 Bruxelles* (1975).

PEDRO ALMODÓVAR (B.1951) SPANISH.
Flamboyant film-maker, whose talent for stylized design and socio-sexual satire is best seen in offbeat offerings like *Women on the Verge of a Nervous Breakdown* (1988).

THEO ANGELOPOULOS (B.1936) GREEK.
Famed for long takes and film trilogies, he mixes myth with politics to explore the lessons of history, most accessibly in *Ulysses' Gaze* (1995).

LUC BESSON (B.1959) FRENCH.
Established with 'cinéma du look' classics like *Subway* (1985) and *The Big Blue* (1988), broke French budget records with his sci-fi blockbuster *The Fifth Element* (1997).

BERTRAND BLIER (B.1939) FRENCH.
Cynical and surreal, he delights in shocking with black comic studies of delinquency, sex and gender politics like *Les Valseuses* (1974) and *Tenue de Soirée* (1986).

CONSTANTIN COSTA-GAVRAS (B.1933) FRENCH.
Greek-born director who began with political thrillers like *Z* (1969), but has since made award-winning pictures in Hollywood, including *Missing* (1982).

MANOEL DE OLIVEIRA (B.1908) PORTUGUESE.
Directing since 1931, his studies of desire, guilt and fear of damnation have earned him auteur status, although the likes of *The Satin Slipper* (1985) are rarely seen outside festivals.

Box-office success has made Claude Lelouch the unsung auteur of French cinema.

MARCO FERRERI (1928–1997) ITALIAN.
Famed for the food satire *La Grande Bouffe* (1973), this savage critic of bourgeois values is at his best exploring the sexual hierarchy, urban alienation and consumerism.

YILMAZ GÜNEY (1937–1984) TURKISH.
This onetime actor's outspoken directorial career landed him in jail. He smuggled out the script for *Yol* (1982), before completing *The Wall* (1984) in France prior to his death.

JUZO ITAMI (1933–1997) JAPANESE.
Debuting with *Death Japanese Style* (1984), he specialized in biting satires on modern Japan, including the 'noodle Western', *Tampopo* (1986) and *A Taxing Woman* (1987).

ABBAS KIAROSTAMI (B.1940) IRANIAN.
One of the few directors to prosper either side of the Islamic Revolution, his simple stories like *The Taste of Cherries* (1996) have a deceptive political and stylistic complexity.

CLAUDE LELOUCH (B.1937) FRENCH.
The populist amidst the new wave artiness, he has scored consistently at the box-office since *A Man and a Woman* (1966) and *Live for Life* (1967).

DAVID LYNCH (B.1946) AMERICAN.

From *Eraserhead* (1978) to *Blue Velvet* (1986) and beyond, this indie icon has inhabited a world all of his own. Yet he excelled himself with the cult TV show *Twin Peaks*.

NIKITA MIKHAILKOV (B.1945) RUSSIAN.

The brother of director Andrei Konchalovsky has made his name with Chekhovian dramas like *Slave to Love* (1976), about early Russian cinema, and the Oscar-winning *Burnt by the Sun* (1994).

ERMANNO OLMI (B.1931) ITALIAN.

This latterday neo-realist forged an international reputation with the office comedy *The Job* (1961) and the moving study of rural life *The Tree of the Wooden Clogs* (1978).

MAURICE PIALAT (B.1925) FRENCH.

This uncompromising auteur has used his gift for bleak realism to focus on outcasts like the working-class slob in *Loulou* (1980) and the tortured priest in *Under Satan's Son* (1987).

FRANCESCO ROSI (B.1922) ITALIAN.

A disciple of neo-realism, he is remembered for hard-hitting exposés of organized crime and corruption like *Salvatore Giuliano* (1962) and *Hands Over the City* (1963).

ALAN RUDOLPH (B.1943) AMERICAN.

An unpredictable auteur, Robert Altman's protégé is nevertheless capable of provocative character dramas like *Choose Me* (1984) and *Mrs Parker and the Vicious Circle* (1994).

Abandon rationality all ye who enter the film world of David Lynch.

RAUL RUIZ (B.1941) CHILEAN.

Personal, political, realist, satirical, traditional and avant-garde – experimental scarcely describes the work of this uniquely cinematic director, who broke through with *The Hypothesis of the Stolen Painting* (1978).

The Taviani brothers – in sync, as always.

CARLOS SAURA (B.1932) SPANISH.

Earned an international reputation during the Franco era for allegories like *The Hunt* (1965). But since best known for such flamenco ballets as *Blood Wedding* (1981) and *Carmen* (1983).

ISTVÁN SZABÓ (B.1938) HUNGARIAN.

As *Confidence* (1979), *Mephisto* (1981) and *Colonel Redl* (1985) demonstrate, few have better used the past to comment on the present.

BERTRAND TAVERNIER (B.1944) FRENCH.

Debuting with *The Watchmaker of St Paul* (1974), this one-time critic has become known for literate films on historical (*Clean Slate*, 1981) and contemporary (*The Bait*, 1994) topics.

VITTORIO (B. 1929) AND PAOLO (B.1931) TAVIANI ITALIAN.

Recalling the neo-realists in *Padre Padrone* (1977), the brothers brought a touch of fantasy to *The Night of San Lorenzo* (1982) and cinematic legend to *Good Morning, Babylon* (1987).

ROGER VADIM (B.1928) FRENCH.

The man who cast Brigitte Bardot in *And God Created Woman* (1956). His non-traditional approach paved the way for the nouvelle vague.

ANDY WARHOL (1927–87) AMERICAN.

Films like *Sleep* (1963) and *Chelsea Girls* (1966) made him the best-known exponent of US undergound cinema.

Film Festival Calendar

If you would like to spend your year wandering from one film festival to the next, it's just about possible. If it's June, it must be Sydney…

JANUARY
Brussels
Clermont-Ferrand, France (shorts)
Gothenburg (non-competitive)
New Delhi (Peacock award)
Rotterdam
Sundance*, Salt Lake City

FEBRUARY
Berlin* (awards Golden Bear)
Fantasporto, Oporto

MARCH
Cleveland, Ohio
Istanbul (awards Golden Tulip)

Oberhausen*, Germany (shorts)
Tampere, Finland (shorts)
Viennale, Vienna (non-competitive)

APRIL
Cannes* (awards Palme d'Or)
Cape Town
Hong Kong (non-competitive)
Houston, Texas
Milan
San Francisco (non-competitive)
Washington (non-competitive)

MAY
Annecy, France (animation)
Cracow (shorts, Golden Dragon awarded)

JUNE
La Rochelle
Melbourne
Munich (non-competitive)*
Sydney
Zagreb (animation)

JULY
Auckland
Jerusalem
Karlovy Vary, Czech Republic*
Moscow*
Philadelphia
Wellington (non-competitive)

AUGUST
Edinburgh (non-competitive)*
Locarno (awards Golden Leopard)*
Montreal*
Toronto (animation)

SEPTEMBER
Birmingham
Cork
Deauville (non-competitive)
Helsinki
New York* (non-competitive)
San Sebastian (awards Golden Shell)
Telluride, Colorado (non-competitive)
Toronto
Vancouver
Venice* (awards Golden Lion)

OCTOBER
Carthage (awards Golden Tanit)
Denver (non-competitive)
Dublin
Ghent, Belgium
Los Angeles
Mannheim
Montpelier
Nîmes (shorts; awards Golden Crocodile)
Ottawa (animation)
Seville
Uppsala, Sweden (awards Jackdaw)
Valencia, Spain
Valladolid, Spain (awards Golden Spike)
Warsaw

NOVEMBER
Chicago (awards Golden Hugo)*
Fort Lauderdale
London (non-competitive)*
Puerto Rico
Rio de Janeiro
Stockholm
Thessalonika (awards Golden Alexander)

DECEMBER
Cairo
Taipei

* = most important film festivals

The Top Twenty

Critics and punters don't always agree on which are the most significant films ever made. Compare and contrast these two lists.

E.T.

CRITICS' ALL-TIME TOP TEN

Chosen every 10 years by a panel of international film-makers and critics for the British film journal Sight and Sound.

1 **Citizen Kane**
   (Orson Welles, 1941)

2 **The Rules of the Game**
   (Jean Renoir, 1939)

3 **Tokyo Story**
   (Yasujiro Ozu, 1953)

4 **Vertigo** *(Alfred Hitchcock, 1958)*

5 **The Searchers**
   (John Ford, 1956)

6 **L'Atalante** *(Jean Vigo, 1934),*

7 **The Passion of Joan of Arc**
   (Carl Dreyer, 1928)

8 **Pather Panchali**
   (Sanjit Ray, 1953)

9 **Battleship Potemkin**
   (Sergei Eisenstein, 1925)

10 **2001: A Space Odyssey**
    (Stanley Kubrick, 1968)

2001: A Space Odyssey

ALL-TIME BOX-OFFICE TOP TEN

1 **Titanic**
   (James Cameron, 1997)

2 **Star Wars**
   (George Lucas, 1977)

3 **E.T. The Extraterrestrial**
   (Steven Spielberg, 1982)

4 **Jurassic Park**
   (Steven Spielberg, 1993)

5 **Men in Black**
   (Barry Sonnenfield, 1997)

6 **The Lost World: Jurassic Park** *(Steven Spielberg, 1997)*

7 **Return of the Jedi**
   (Richard Marquand, 1983)

8 **Independence Day**
   (Roland Emmerich, 1996)

9 **The Empire Strikes Back**
   (Irvin Kershner, 1980)

10 **The Lion King** *(Roger Allen, Roger Minikoff, 1994)*

Titanic: first to $1 billion.

Crib Sheet

A selection of terms that crop up in the text.

ANIMATION

The art of bringing inanimate objects to life on the screen. See pages 50–1.

AUTEUR

An artist rather than a jobbing director: someone who brings his own vision and personality to a picture, rather than just mechanically filming the actors delivering their own scripted lines.

AVANT-GARDE

A non-commercial or experimental film or film-maker.

BACKLOT

The area at the rear of a studio where full-size or scale exterior sets are mounted. Most Hollywood studios had their own western or downtown street, which they re-dressed for different pictures. Also common were castles and European town squares.

Gary Cooper walks alone in *High Noon*.

BIOPIC

The screen biography of an actual person.

BLOCKBUSTER

A film that cost a packet to produce and promote in the expectation of a whopping box-office return.

B MOVIE

A cheap, quickly made film shown before the big picture. See pages 52–3, and 'quota quickies' on page 56.

Kirk Douglas shapes up in *Spartacus*.

CAHIERS DU CINÉMA

Founded by André Bazin in 1947, this most influential of film journals played a key role in the French new wave – not only by promoting auteur theory, but also by launching the careers of future directors like François Truffaut, Jean-Luc Godard, Jacques Rivette, Claude Chabrol and Eric Rohmer.

CINÉMA VÉRITÉ

A documentary style, in which a handheld camera is used to record events as inobtrusively as possible. However, the director is often audible and/or visible, as an interviewer or commentator.

COMPUTER-GENERATED IMAGERY (CGI)

Special effect imagery generated by computer, like the dinosaurs in *Jurassic Park*.

Computer-generated dinosaurs in *Jurassic Park*.

CLOSE-UP

A shot in which a face or object fills most of the screen.

CROSS-CUTTING

The method of editing together shots depicting two or more simultaneous actions.

DAY FOR NIGHT

The technique of shooting in daylight using filters or underexposed film to achieve the illusion of darkness.

DEEP FOCUS

The method of composing a shot so that all areas of the image are in sharp focus.

DISSOLVE

An editing device in which a concluded scene is slowly replaced on the screen by the next.

DISTRIBUTOR

The person or company who persuades the exhibitor to show in their cinemas films made by the producer.

DOCUMENTARY

A film that tackles real events, people, places or abstract themes in a factual rather than a fictional way.

DOLLY

Silent, hydraulically powered moving platform, which supports the camera and its operator during short dolly or travelling shots. It's pushed or driven by a dolly grip.

EXPRESSIONISM

An artistic movement that expressed thoughts or emotions via exaggerated or distorted shapes. Often appllied to German horror films of the early 1920s.

Designer Expressionism: *Nosferatu*, the remake.

FADE-IN

The gradual appearance of an image on the screen. In the case of a fade-out, the image recedes into darkness.

FEATURE FILM

Any film running for more than one hour, although the average length is 90 minutes.

FILM D'ART

The term applied to the lavish costume dramas starring the leading French stars of the 1910s.

FILM NOIR

Crime melodramas populated by any combination of femmes fatales, hapless war veterans, petty racketeers, corrupt cops and debased members of the Establishment. Hollywood noir was in vogue between 1941 and 1955, although there have been several latterday revivals.

A dope gets duped in *Double Indemnity*.

FLASHBACK

A shot or scene depicting events that have occurred earlier in the story – either on or off the screen.

FRAME

A single shot on a strip of film, or the margins of a screen image.

FREEZE FRAME

A shot in which the action stops abruptly while the image remains static on the screen.

A star is born:
Mel Gibson in *Mad Max*.

GENRE

A group of films linked by such recurrent recognizable conventions as plot, character, setting, themes, techniques and stars. The main genres are comedy, crime (including gangsters and film noir), horror, the musical, sci-fi and the western, although other convenient groupings include action/adventure, the costume melodrama, thrillers, war films and the woman's picture.

INDEPENDENT FILM

Indie films are those made without the backing of a major studio or production company.

JUMP CUT

An abrupt breach in the action made either by removing a few frames or by stopping the action and recommencing shooting from a different camera angle. The purpose of a jump cut is to disrupt the flow of the story and draw attention to the film-making process.

KIDPIX

Films aimed at younger audiences.

LOCATION SHOOTING

Any filming that happens outside the studio confines.

LONG SHOT

A shot in which objects or vistas are shown at a considerable distance from the camera.

LONG TAKES

A sequence filmed continuously from a stationary or moving camera which is then shown on-screen without any cross-cutting.

MISE EN SCÈNE

Meaning 'putting in the scene', it initially described everything contained in a shot – the action, set, props, lighting, costumes and make-up. It's since come to mean the technique of recording long takes in deep focus from a moving camera in order to establish the mood and atmosphere of a scene without resort to editing.

Joan Crawford setting the scene in *Mildred Pierce* (1945).

MONTAGE
An editing technique pioneered by Soviet film-makers of the silent era, in which images are rapidly cross-cut for narrative, emotional or symbolic effect.

NEO-REALISM
The term applied to films which used real locations, natural lighting and non-professional performers to explore the social and economic condition of post-war Italy although it has spread worldwide.

NEWSREEL
A factual film comprising footage of topical news and sporting events. Running 10–20 minutes, it was shown before the big picture, although there were also separate newsreel cinemas. Charles Pathé showed the first in New York in 1911 and they remained popular until after World War II.

NEW WAVE
The name given to any film movement that departs from tradition. World cinema was overrun with them in the 1960s following the French New Wave.

NOUVELLE VAGUE
The French New Wave.

PERSISTENCE OF VISION
The brain's ability to retain an image for a fleeting second after it has vanished from sight – without which movies simply wouldn't work!

PROP
Any object – from clocks to guns – that helps drive the plot or brings realism to a scene.

SET
The film equivalent of a stage complete with props and scenery.

SHORT
Any film lasting under 30 minutes.

SUPERIMPOSITION
The presence of two or more images in a single frame.

SYNCHRONIZE
The process of combining sound and vision so that a character's voice and lip movements occur simultaneously or are in sync.

TAKE
Any single continuous shot recorded by the camera.

Teenpix: no sitting on the fence, you either love 'em or loathe 'em.

TEENPIX
Films aimed at the teenage market.

WOMAN'S PICTURE
Films aimed predominantly at a female audience.

ZOOM
A shot taken from a stationary camera that gives the impression of sudden movement towards or away from an object.

Jimmy Cagney with trademark props.

Index

PHOTOGRAPHIC CREDITS

AKG, London, p.26.
All other photographs courtesy of the Kobal
Collection.

WITH THANKS TO:

Disney Enterprises Ltd © for pp.50, 51, 130.
A.I.P., Akira, Bryna/Universal, Cady/Piscina;
Carolco; Ceskoslovensky/Barrandon/Carlopon;
Cine del Dula/Pleylyre; Columbia; Edison;
E.M.I.; Epic; Flaherty; Gaumont;
Gaumont/British; Goskino; Govt. of W. Bengal.
Jan Chapman Productions/Ciby 2000, Ladd
Company; Light Storm Entertainments; London
Films; Lucas Films Ltd; Lucas Films/20th
Century Fox; Lucas Films/Paramount.
Lux/De L'Aurentis; M.G.M./Pathé; Miramax;
Mosfilm; Newline/Cinema; Newline/Darkhorse;
Newline/Newline Productions; Orion;
Paramount; Paris Film/Five Film; PEA Artistes
Associes; Picnic/B.E.F./Aus. Film Commission;
Propaganda/Polygram; R.K.O., Rank; Riame-
Pathé; Road Movies/Argos Films/W.D.R.;
Selznick/M.G.M.; Society General De Films;
Stanley Kramer; Svensk Film Industri; Tigon;
Trio/Albatross/W.D.R. Tristar; U.F.A.; United
Artists, Universal, Warner Bros; Woodfall Ass.
British; Working Title/Channel 4;
Zoetrope/U.A.